MW01394277

The Spirit of Attack

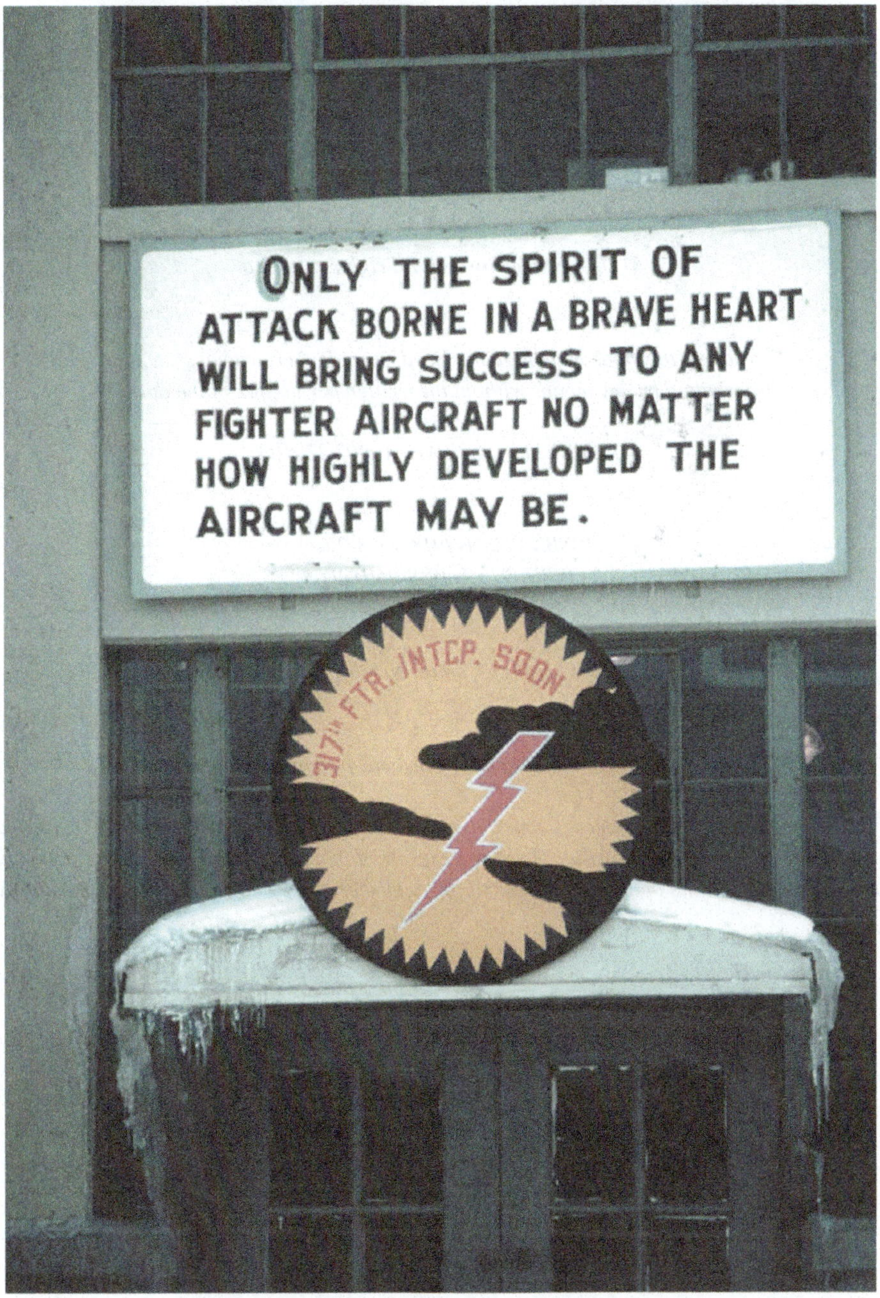
ONLY THE SPIRIT OF
ATTACK BORNE IN A BRAVE HEART
WILL BRING SUCCESS TO ANY
FIGHTER AIRCRAFT NO MATTER
HOW HIGHLY DEVELOPED THE
AIRCRAFT MAY BE.
317th FTR. INTCP. SQDN

Fighter Pilot Stories

by
Bruce Gordon

AuthorHouse™ LLC
1663 Liberty Drive
Bloomington, IN 47403
www.authorhouse.com
Phone: 1-800-839-8640

© *2014 Bruce Gordon. All rights reserved.*

No part of this book may be reproduced, stored in a retrieval system, or transmitted by any means without the written permission of the author.

Published by AuthorHouse 02/27/2014

ISBN: 978-1-4918-4603-2 (sc)
ISBN: 978-1-4918-4604-9 (e)

Library of Congress Control Number: 2013923787

This book is printed on acid-free paper.

Because of the dynamic nature of the Internet, any web addresses or links contained in this book may have changed since publication and may no longer be valid. The views expressed in this work are solely those of the author and do not necessarily reflect the views of the publisher, and the publisher hereby disclaims any responsibility for them.

The Spirit of Attack

"Spirit of Attack" sign over the entrance to the 317th Fighter
Interceptor Squadron Elmendorf AFB, Anchorage, Alaska in 1964

The "Spirit of Attack" is quoted from Adolf Galland's book, "The First and the Last". He was one of Germany's top aces and became Commander of German fighter forces in WW II. This quote was the motto of my fighter squadron in Alaska, my guide for 20 years of flying with the US Air Force, and the title for this book.

I flew 132 combat missions in Vietnam and was awarded the Distinguished Flying Cross for close support for US ground troops in bad weather in mountainous terrain. This book has over 40 first-person stories plus over 90 photos and illustrations. Some photos were taken from my own fighter cockpit with my two hands on the camera, while flying the airplane with the stick between my knees. Some of these show volcanoes in Alaska and my own bombs exploding in Vietnam.

Three stories are contributed by my fighter pilot friends. Harry Shumate tells of combat in Korea; Ray Janes tells of being a Forward Air Controller (FAC) in Vietnam, and Phil Payne tells of flying in support of a nuclear weapons test.

The last story is a WW II bombing raid by P-38 fighters of the First Fighter Wing against the oil fields of Ploesti, Romania. I was Editor of their newsletter for several years. I spoke with pilots who had flown on that mission, and read their reports. I found a story by a Romanian pilot who had flown against us that day. I set the American reports against the Romanian report to get a rare view of a battle from opposing cockpits. Pilots in dogfights seldom agree on what happened -- and these stories differ in details -- but it shows that pilots from both sides had the "Spirit of Attack" and fought hard for their countries.

Contents

Beginnings 1
1942—Refugees 3
Back to Hawaii—by Convoy 3

Pilot Training 5
Primary Pilot Training 5
Basic Jet Training Laredo AFB, Texas 8
Advanced Interceptor Training 10
Moody AFB, Valdosta, Georgia 10

Fighter Pilot 12
Geiger Field, Spokane, Washington 12
A Hero—or a Murderer? 13
Design Deficiencies Kill 14
Alaska—and the Spirit of Attack 15
Cuban Missile Crisis—seen from Alaska 15
Wingman Bailout 17
Russian Bombers Over Alaska 18
Unidentified Flying Objects (UFOs) 19
Military Exercises 19
Icy Runways 21
Alaskan Cold 21
Electronic Countermeasures (ECM) 22
"Battle Stations" and "Silent Scramble" 22
Kamikaze 22
Iditarod 23
Landing Short 24
Murder at Galena 24

Arrest that Policeman!	25
Alaska Earthquake	25
Pilotless F-102	27

Selfridge AFB 29

Night Flight	29
Bomarc Kill	31
MACE Kill	33
Flight Test	35
Supersonic Target	36
I become a UFO	37
Captain Eddie Rickenbacker in WW I	37

Aerial Combat Tactics 39

Tumbling the F-106	40
F-106 vs. F-104	40
Aerodynamics of Combat	41
Korean Air Defense	43
Korean Mission	43
Overconfidence	45
F-106 vs. F-102	46
F-106 vs. F-4, Low-Speed Dogfight	46
F-106 vs. F-4, Low Altitude, High Speed	47
F-106 vs. F-4, High Altitude, High Speed	47
F-106 vs. F-4 "Coco Scramble"	49
Angela Orphanage	49
Something Big	50

Wake Island 51

Vietnam War 53

Jungle Survival School	54

Tuy Hoa Air Base, Vietnam	54
Phan Rang Air Base, Vietnam	55
Fire on the Water	55
The Battle of Prey-Totung	56
Night Weather	61
Low Fuel	61
Enemy Fire	62
Friendly Fire	63
Inflight Refueling	64
Bomb Fuzes	65
Thanh Hoa Bridge	66
The Dog's Head	67
Troops in Contact	68
Poem—"An Hour before I Fly"	69
Distinguished Flying Cross	**71**
Saigon — 7th Air Force Headquarters	71
Rabies (Hydrophobia)	71
R&R in Hawaii	73
Last Flight	74
Conclusions	74
Contributed Stories	**76**
Harry Shumate Stories	76
Korean War Combat	76
Probable MiG Kill	77
Close Call	77
Barracks happening between flights	78
Ground Attack	79
Shot Down	80

    Bailout and Rescue..81

Phil Payne Stories..83
    Atomic Bomb Test..83

    Supersonic Flight 86

    F-102 Missile Firing 86

Ray Janes Stories..89
    A 94th FIS ORI 89

    A Shaky Flight 90

    A Small Error 90

    It's A Crate! 91

    Vietnam Stories..92

    The Day I Blew Up A Mountain 95

WW II: Mission to Remember..98
    The 1st & 82nd Fighter Groups over Ploesti..98

    The View from a P-38 99

    The Romanian View of the Battle 103

Beginnings

I was born in the Philippine Islands in 1934 where my father worked for the Eastman Kodak Company. I had an older brother and a younger sister, all born in the Philippines. This was the middle of the Great Depression, and we had very little money. The cost of living was so low that we had Filipino servants at very little cost and held wonderful birthday parties. Home movies made us look rich. My father wore a white cotton suit to work every day, and wore a cotton "dinner jacket" (tuxedo) when he and Mom went to the Polo Club for events. He had several suits, and our servants washed and ironed them every night. The weather was hot and we had mosquito nets over our beds because malaria and dengue fever were common. In this photo, my father and I watch my big brother serve tea.

In 1936 my father was given "home leave" and took us to Kodak's home office in Rochester, NY, via the Suez Canal, France, and England, on the German steamer *"MV Sharnhorst"*. On this German ship he heard that another world war was likely, and that Japan might be allied with Germany. When he got to Rochester, my father told management about his concerns and asked for a transfer to a safe location, farther from Japan. We returned to the Philippines across the Pacific, so I completed my first trip around the world while I was 2 years old!

Back in the Philippines, life was good but the talk of war increased. My father repeated his request for transfer to a safe location. In 1939 World War II started in Europe, and our family finally transferred to the relative safety of Hawaii. My father was Assistant Manager of Kodak Hawaii, and I visited him in his office. Kodak sold cameras and film to tourists, and arranged for free hula dances because the tourists used so much film.

Sunday, December 7, 1941 dawned peacefully. I was seven years old and remember events clearly. My older brother and I took our BB guns and went to the beach where we shot crabs. Suddenly my mother came running, calling for us to come home immediately. The radio kept saying: "The Japanese are attacking Pearl Harbor. This is not a drill. This is the real McCoy!". My father drove to the Kodak office in Honolulu and watched from the roof, seeing smoke billowing from Pearl Harbor. Our own antiaircraft shells were falling in Honolulu, setting fires and killing a number of civilians. He came home and we watched as the US Army reacted to the attack by deploying troops to defend the beaches. Some aircraft flew low over our house; one was a B-17 bomber which happened to arrive from California in the middle of the attack, and was desperately trying to shake off Zero fighters and find a place to land. Mom was serving lunch when we heard machine gun fire almost in our back yard! Mom was so startled that she spilled a bowl of peas all over the table. The Army had dug a machine gun nest at the treeline on our beach, and the soldiers were testing their guns. Dad filled bags with sand and made a place for us to hide under our laundry sink. He got buckets of sand to fight fires, as we heard that incendiary bombs were made of phosphorous and could not be extinguished by water. That night started with full blackout. No lights, not even cigarettes, were permitted where they could be seen. My younger sister went up to her bedroom and turned on a light, which shone through a window and caused a crisis! Our Japanese neighbor went to his refrigerator to get a late-night snack—the refrigerator light flashed on, and an Army patrol nearly shot our neighbor as a spy!

Christmas Day, 1941 ended our childhood innocence — we were soon at sea in a convoy consisting of three fast passenger ships and ten defensive ships—a "fast convoy" which could cruise at about 20 knots. A submerged submarine traveled at 7 knots. A fast convoy need fear only submarines which happened to be lucky enough to be in front of the zigzagging convoy. Postwar intelligence tells us that five Japanese submarines were stationed near Pearl Harbor—one was sunk by aircraft on December 10th, so four were still near Pearl Harbor when we left on December 25th. Our course was zigzag, so they were probably not in position to attack.

The Spirit of Attack

The ship was overcrowded — the swimming pool had been drained and filled with bunk beds — and we had to wear life jackets all the time or use them as pillows when we slept. We had frequent lifeboat drills. The warships test-fired their guns and dropped depth charges to be sure they worked. A US submarine cruised with us briefly so everyone could see how hard a real submarine was to see in the open ocean. It was hot below decks, and the December winds blew cold when we slept on deck. We kids had only our light Aloha shirts and short pants, no coats. We were shivering with cold on New Years Eve as we sailed under the Golden Gate Bridge into San Francisco. Everyone sang, "California, here we come — right back where we started from". We had survived the first convoy out of Pearl Harbor after the attack.

Pan American Airways flew their famous flying boat, the Pan American Clipper, to Manila in 1935. My mother took my brother and me to see it -- it was probably the first airplane I ever saw.

Pan American built a refueling stop for the Clipper at Wake Island, which was uninhabited because there was no natural source of fresh water. Pan American built cement catch-basins for rainwater. The U.S. Marines moved a small force onto Wake. After attacking Pearl Harbor, the Japanese fleet attacked and captured Wake Island. The gallant defense of Wake Island by a few Marines has almost been lost in history. After the Marines drove off the first landing with heavy losses, the Japanese landed at night. The Marines' last message was: "Enemy on island. Situation in doubt."

December 7th, 1941. The Japanese hit in two waves of planes. They did considerable damage, but canceled a second attack because they did not know where the US aircraft carriers were. The US carriers were at sea delivering fighter planes to Wake Island and Johnson Island, and could not have influenced the battle. The Japanese failure to follow up their initial success was a major blunder.

Several times, Japanese commanders turned cautious after their initial successes and failed to take risks which might have led to significant victories. Their commanders had the "Bushido" Spirit, but not the Spirit of Attack. They turned back when faced with uncertainty. US Navy photos

Page 2 — **Bruce Gordon Stories**

1942—Refugees

New Years Eve found us shivering with cold on the dock. We had no warm clothes and no home. The American Red Cross gave us warm clothes and found us room at the Sir Francis Drake Hotel in San Francisco. Mom's friend Eleanor Breed came to the Sir Francis Drake Hotel and helped us out. When my mother later died 33 years later, Eleanor and my father married and Eleanor became my stepmother. Family friends can be helpful over many years.

The cost of living in San Francisco was high and in a few days we were on the way to Tucson, Arizona, where my mother thought the cost of living would be lower. She rented a house near Sam Hughes Elementary School. Her letters of the time refer to the high cost of living as nearby Davis Monthan Air Force Base grew into a major installation. This was the end of the Great Depression; Dad's pay was low. Kodak had no provisions for families separated by war. Dad's pay was sent to Hawaii, and he re-sent it by check to my mother, whose address was changing. He abandoned our house, lived in his office, and sent her almost all his money. Her letters from Tucson say she received a check and she was surprised that he had sent so much.

We walked to and from Sam Hughes School. One day it was pouring rain at lunchtime, and I foolishly went out in the rain. I came back to school after lunch and all afternoon I sat in wet clothes, coming down with a very bad cold. By nightfall it turned into an incredibly painful earache. This was before the days of antibiotics, so all Mom could do was to give me aspirin and put warm oil in my ear. My temperature rose to the danger point, and Mom called a doctor. Soon I was in the hospital with pneumonia. I remember being in an oxygen tent. The only medicines were sulfa drugs, which had many side effects, probably attacking my liver. I was near death, and Mom came to my bedside to talk to me. I was in a private room (my other hospital stays were usually in "wards" with many patients), so she was getting me the best care possible. I heard the nurses talking and they said that I was dying. The hospital costs must have been very high, as my mother's letters said that she'd rather pay my hospital bills than have clothes or jewels, as her children were her jewels. I recovered, but was weak.

Mom took us to Mexico because the cost of living was less and she hoped that we would learn Spanish. It was a disaster. I nearly died of a liver disease. An American doctor was visiting, and she asked him to look at me. He said: "I don't know what is wrong with the boy, but he is dying. You must take him to an American hospital, but he's too sick to travel". Mom immediately put us on a train back so I could get medical help. The trip back was very rough, as I was terribly sick. Once in an American hospital, I recovered my strength slowly.

Back to Hawaii—by Convoy

1942 ended with the family separated. Dad telephoned us from Hawaii once a month, for three minutes. The American victory at the Battle of Midway in June 1942 convinced him that the US would win the war, and he started making plans for our return to Hawaii. He came to Tucson in July 1943 to get us. We all went to San Francisco and took two rooms in the Canterbury Hotel. Dad had a high priority to get back to Hawaii, so in two days he was on a boat headed back. The rest of us remained in the Canterbury Hotel for nine months, expecting to ship out at any time. The manager of the Canterbury Hotel tried to enforce a hotel policy that allowed guests to stay for a maximum of two weeks, but Mom said we had no place to go and the manager let us stay. My mother got very sick and went to the hospital, and we three kids were taken care of by family friends and even by complete strangers who volunteered to help. My brother and I got into trouble as unsupervised boys tend to do. We got on the roof of the Canterbury Hotel and threw pebbles down on people who sunbathing or reading in the patio below. The hotel manager was merciful and did not throw us out of the hotel.

In April 1944 we finally embarked on another convoy and headed for Hawaii. Bob and I were with the men in a forward hold of the ship, and the bunks were four high. I was nine years old. Climbing up to my bunk was a real task, and I was afraid of falling out. We sailed out of the Golden Gate and met the heavy swells of the open sea; soon many men were seasick and were cursing constantly. Meals were served on stamped metal trays in a crowded galley. At meal times we could meet Mom and Ann; they were in the aft hold with the women, and their experience was similarly bad. The weather was getting warmer. We were happy to get to Hawaii.

San Francisco, January 1942. Mom knew we were leaving Hawaii and brought her best clothes. We three kids had never owned warm clothes. San Francisco was cold in January. The American Red Cross gave us warm clothes, which didn't fit too well. My brother wears the Red Cross clothes in the photo of him with my mother. My sister and I are wearing our light Hawaiian clothes that we wore on Christmas Day to visit our friends.. I vividly remember how cold I was.

We remained in Hawaii, going to Punahou School, and had a house on Mount Tantalus overlooking Honolulu. Our home had its own bomb shelter. After the war, Dad was assigned to Kodak China, and we went to Hong Kong until the Communists got too close and business dried up. We returned to the USA just before the Korean War began. The conflict with Communism was very much in our minds as we went to college, and I joined the AFROTC.

At the end of WW II we got ready to dismantle our family bomb shelter. We took this photo for a Christmas card. My brother carries a gas mask. I'm in the background with the "For Rent" sign on the bomb shelter.

Pilot Training

I considered a career in Conservation (now called "Environmental Science") but was also interested in world history and politics. Tufts U. in Massachusetts had an Air Force Reserve Officer Training Corps (AFROTC) with a course in Geopolitics. It also had paid $47.88 per month as a subsistence ration, and I needed the money. I became very interested in global air power. I applied for and was accepted into pilot training.

Summer, 1955 — AFROTC summer camp was at Ethan Allen AFB, Winooski, Vermont. We learned to shoot rifles and pistols; I was always a very good shot. It was a tough camp, both physically and mentally — we did a lot of physical exercises, running and marching. This photo shows me (front row, left) with fellow AFROTC Cadets at the end of camp — we were healthy and tanned! The AFROTC gave me a commission as a Second Lieutenant when I graduated from Tufts in June 1956. My orders were to report to Lackland AFB, San Antonio, Texas, in August. The Korean War had ended in a dangerously tense truce. President Eisenhower was in the White House and the Cold War threatened to get hot.

I reported to Lackland AFB on August 24, 1956 and began a 20-year career. I transferred to Graham Air Base in Marianna, Florida for Basic Pilot Training. Graham was a pleasant place, run by civilian contractors who taught us to fly. I started with the T-34 trainer, and I soloed after 10 hours of dual training. I learned basic aerobatics and emergency procedures. I then upgraded to the T-28A, which was much larger and more powerful than the T-34; a version of the T-28 was later used by the South Vietnamese and others as a ground attack fighter. For the first time, I became interested in the mechanics of engines and the design of constant-speed propellers. I became interested in aircraft maintenance, which led to my secondary Air Force career as an aircraft maintenance officer. In July 1957 I went to Laredo AFB in southern Texas and flew the T-33 for Basic jet training. I was awarded my Wings in December 1957. I loved flying and decided to make it my career.

Primary Pilot Training

Graham Air Base in Marianna, Florida was a beautiful place to learn to fly. Instead of straight, right-angle streets, its streets wandered among groves of trees, like a civilian community. Our quarters looked more like a motel than barracks. We had student officers (most were 2nd Lieutenants, like myself) and Aviation Cadets, who would receive their Commissions as officers if and when they got their Wings. We had foreign pilot trainees: Germans and Thai. It was interesting to train with the Germans, who (like us) could clearly remember World War II. We got along well, as now we were allies in the Cold War.

Primary Pilot Training started with the T-34 trainer. Made by Beechcraft, it was related to their Beechcraft Bonanza private plane. It had a 225-hp engine and was nice for aerobatics.

After the T-34 we flew the T-28A trainer with a powerful engine; some versions could carry guns and light bombs. The engine and propeller were complex, and gave the T-28 good range. We learned to navigate, both day and night, using dead reckoning and maps. We learned instrument flying and could make approaches to airports using radio beacons.

Next I flew the T-33, a trainer version of our first jet fighter, the F-80 Shooting Star, with a top speed of about seven-tenths the speed of sound. We wore oxygen masks and flew as high as 40,000 feet, much higher than propeller planes could fly. Jets went fast, but consumed fuel rapidly; we learned to conserve fuel to get the most range out of our aircraft. I got my Wings on Dec 5, 1957.

Our instructors were civilians with WW II experience. They trained us in the military way of flying: checklists, careful preflight inspections, precise radio calls. Ground school had excellent classes on engines, hydraulics and electrical systems. These classes gave me my first real understanding of systems, and my interest deepened over the years until I was an Aircraft Maintenance Officer at the end of my Air Force career.

Graham was a pleasant place to learn to fly. The mild Florida weather was punctuated by strong thunderstorms, and the nearby swamps were great places for me to hunt snakes with my .22 caliber pistol. The Aviation Cadets would sing marching songs as they marched to classes or to the flight line; those songs ring in my ears today: "I'm engaged to marry soon, Honey, Honey, Babe, Babe. I'm engaged to marry soon, Honey, Oh Baby mine. I'm afraid to get undressed, 'cause MARY's tattooed on my chest, Honey, Oh Baby mine. Go to your left, your right, your left" etc., for many verses.

I'm getting ready to fly the T-34

We had eight to ten hours of dual time in the T-34 with an instructor, then we got to solo. My instructor, Mr. Payne, was a good man. He was tough but fair. We learned basic aerobatics and to spin the T-34. A spin is dangerous. The nose goes almost straight down, the wing outside the turn moves faster and generates lift, while the wing inside the turn moves more slowly and generates less lift, so the tendency is for the spin to get faster and faster, to "wrap up" tightly. A pilot's normal reaction is to pull back on the stick to get out of the steep dive, which is exactly the wrong thing to do. "Pull the stick all the way back, if you want to go all the way down", we were told. In the early days of flying, the spin always ended in a crash. Finally, Glenn Curtiss of the Curtiss-Wright Airplane Company pushed the stick forward, and recovered from the spin. A heavy jet fighter can get into violent spins and my units lost several fighters to spins.

We put the T-34 into a deliberate spin by reducing power and slowing down, gradually pulling the nose up as we approached a stall. The plane shuddered as it stalled, and the nose dropped down. At that moment we pulled the stick all the way back and stepped on either rudder pedal, sending the plane into a violent spin. We let it spin for a couple of violent turns as the world spun around us, and the instructor would command: "RECOVER!" Quick rudder against the spin to stop the rotation, pop the stick smartly forward, and you're suddenly in a steep dive. Don't pull the stick back too fast or you'll hit a "secondary stall" and the plane might snap into a secondary spin in the opposite direction than the first spin. Instead, let the plane dive for a couple of seconds to make sure you have good flying speed, then smoothly pull out of the dive. The T-34 usually fell about 500 to 800 feet in a spin; later, in jet fighters, it took almost 10,000 feet to recover from a spin.

I was ready to solo, and went with my instructor for a last dual flight. After some aerobatics, we headed back toward the field and I descended to traffic pattern altitude, 1,000 feet above the ground. Suddenly the instructor said "I'VE GOT IT" and took the controls. He chopped the power, yanked up the nose and kicked rudder. The plane snapped into a spin. He let it turn a couple of times as we fell toward the ground. "YOU'VE GOT IT. RECOVER!" he barked and released the controls. I grabbed the controls, kicked rudder and snapped the stick forward of neutral. The plane came out of the spin, going straight down toward the ground! I gently pulled back on the stick and came out of the dive, close to the ground. There had been no altitude left to recover from a secondary spin—my instructor had bet our lives that I would recover correctly.

We continued back to the field and landed. "Take it up again, get three touch-and-go landings, then park it" he said. My instructor climbed out of the plane, and I taxied to the takeoff position. I was alone—I was going to solo! I got a green light from Mobile Control, lined up with the runway and applied power. The plane rolled forward and lifted into the air — the exhilarating feeling of freedom surged through me. I completed my practice landings and parked my plane. As I got out, my friends dumped ice water on me. That's the traditional honor for a pilot who has just soloed!

The Spirit of Attack

One of my friends was flying solo over the Florida swamps when he hit a vulture. The big bird crashed through the plexiglass canopy into the cockpit—and was still alive! He radioed that he had an emergency, and was fighting with a vulture in his cockpit. We watched as he came in for a wobbly landing and the fire trucks and ambulance chased the T-34 as it came to a stop. The medics scrambled to the cockpit and found him beating on the bloody vulture with his flashlight! The medics gave him sedatives and sent him to bed for the rest of the day.

After more solo flying and check flights we upgraded to the T-28 trainer. The T-28 had four times as much power as the T-34, with many complicated controls. There were cowl flaps to cool the engine, propeller controls and mixture controls to get the best performance out of the plane. Soon we were using only instruments to fly "under the hood", a canvas cover which kept the student pilot from looking outside. Then we started night flying, and navigated across the southern USA checking the lights of cities against our maps and finding where to go.

The T-28. I'm kneeling in front; my instructor and two students are standing.

One night we had twenty T-28s airborne with solo pilots on a night round-robin navigation flight. A huge thunderstorm headed toward our base and the Commander radioed for all of us to return to base and land immediately. We got back just as the rain was starting to pour down. One plane did not return! The thunderstorm pounded the base, and our calls to the lost plane were unanswered. Hours passed and hope dimmed for our lost comrade. The storm gradually moved on, and we heard a noise — a T-28 was coming in to land! He had had complete electrical power failure and lost his radios, lights, and navigation equipment. He tried to get back to the base, but saw the thunderstorm covering the base. He turned south toward the Gulf of Mexico, leaned out his fuel mixture to get maximum endurance from the engine and flew in slow circles around a small town while he watched the thunderstorm slowly cross over our base. When the thunderstorm passed and he could see the lights of the base again, he came back and landed. By flying in circles over a town, he did not get lost and was able to find his way back without any navigation equipment. That's a man really using his head to get out of a bad situation!

Basic Jet Training
Laredo AFB, Texas

I volunteered for jet fighter training and went to Laredo AFB in southern Texas for the T-33, a trainer version of our first combat jet, the F-80. The jet engine is simpler and more reliable than the piston engines, and we flew much faster and flew so high (almost 40,000 feet) that we always wore helmets and oxygen masks. We spent hours "under the hood" learning instrument flying. It was 1957, after the Korean War and before the Berlin Wall, and America was gradually cutting back on its military. Pressure was increasing to "wash out" (flunk) student pilots because there weren't enough fighters for us to fly. I worked hard to stay in fighters.

Formation flying washed out a lot of pilots. The jet engine was slow to respond to throttle changes, so you had to anticipate the need for power. The clean jet aircraft would not decelerate quickly if you were going too fast, and you had to reduce power early or you'd go past your leader. Staying in close formation was a constant struggle of adding and taking off power.

During formation takeoffs, everyone would hold the brakes, run up to 100% power and check the engines. Lead would then reduce to 98% power (in case the wingman fell back and needed to catch up) and check to see if everyone was ready.

He'd tilt back his head, then nod forward sharply and release brakes. We would roll down the runway together. At 2,000 feet down the runway, lead would check our speed against expected acceleration to be sure our engines were producing enough thrust. That point was critical — if something was wrong, we could still chop power and stop on the runway. From then on, we were committed to fly or die. At about 100 knots (115 mph) lead would raise his nose off the runway. Matching his aircraft, we would lift off together. We'd watch his flaps and would raise our flaps as he raised his. Communication was mostly through hand signals. We were close enough to see hand signals clearly if he held his gloved hand against his white helmet. Later, in Vietnam, hand signals were harder to see because we had camoflaged helmets.

We would break off formation and then rejoin. Lead would hold a specified speed (usually 250 knots) and start a turn with a 30° bank. To join, we'd drop slightly below him and stay inside his turn, also holding 250 knots. Because we were inside the turn, the circumfrence of our turn was less than his, and we would catch up during the turn. If we were catching up too fast, we'd slip under him to the outside of the turn, and then we'd be on the bigger circle and would drop back. We didn't change power until we were pretty well in close formation. I got pretty good at it, and could "hang tight" while lead did aerobatics.

I was at Mobile Control when I saw my first aircraft accident. My job was to be sure that the planes were ready for flight (speed brakes up, flaps set to 30 degrees, canopy locked, not dripping fluids). Two T-33s lined up for takeoff. The lead was a solo pilot trainee on his first formation flight as leader, and the second plane was dual with an instructor in the back seat. They released brakes and started takeoff roll together. When the moment came to raise the nose off the runway, lead pulled back too far and his nose rose steeply while his wheels were still on the ground. He was now "behind the power curve" . The nose-high attitude had so much aereodynamic drag that the aircraft couldn't accelerate to flying speed. His instructor yelled on the radio to get his nose down, but the student continued nose-high, behind the power curve, and began to drift off the side of the runway onto the dirt. The instructor kept his own nose in the correct position and accelerated, passing the lead plane and continuing a normal takeoff. The student lead, with his nose high in the air, drifted off the runway and ran through the dirt, kicking up a huge cloud of dust. In an attempt to get airborne the student retracted his landing gear and the plane bellied into the dirt at about 100 mph. The plane skidded to a stop in a huge cloud of dust. The student knew he had to escape from the plane, so he blew his canopy. I saw the canopy go almost straight up, then fall back on the aircraft doing considerable damage. The pilot jumped out of the plane and started running, but he had forgotten to shut off the engine. The engine was still at full power as a fire truck pulled up and a fireman ran to the cockpit and shut off the engine. The student was still running away, so an ambulance chased him down and gave him a ride back home. He had flunked formation flying!

BEWARE OF BLAST! While in Texas for flight training, I wrote letters to my college girlfriend (and future wife) Midge Canty. We did not agree about some things, especially religion. I sent her this photo, then when I had a strong point to make, I wrote "Beware of Blast" on the back of the envelope. We finally settled some issues. She flew down to Laredo, Texas and we got engaged.

My instructor, 1st Lt. Weisenborn, and my fellow student, 2nd Lt Dwyer, ready to taxi out for a flight. Each pilot sat on an ejection seat which was basically a 40 mm cannon shell which could throw the pilot up high enough to clear the tail in the event of a bailout. The canopy also had an explosive charge to blow it off before the pilots ejected. If the canopy would not blow off, the pilots could eject right through the plexiglass canopy.

Advanced Interceptor Training

Moody AFB, Valdosta, Georgia

I got my Wings in December 1957, and was assigned to fighter interceptor training at Moody AFB. The F-86L was an interceptor version of the famous F-86 which won the air battles of the Korean War. Its radar had a range of about 6 miles, and an afterburner which allowed it to go supersonic in a vertical dive. When breaking the "sound barrier", the plane would briefly roll to left or right. It was armed with twenty-four 2.5" "Mighty Mouse" unguided rockets. It was a true all-weather fighter. Its computer would bring the fighter on a 90-degree beam attack on the bomber, and at a range of 500 feet would fire all 24 rockets in a shotgun pattern.

The F-86L was advanced for its day. Its search radar gave data to an analog computer system which could compute a beam (90°) attack and show a circle and dot on the radar screen. The pilot would fly to put the dot in the center of the circle until the computer fired the unguided rockets. After firing the rockets, the fighter might pass within 50 feet of the target. This got hairy when the target was big, like the huge B-36 bomber. The rudder of the B-36 stuck up so high that we'd come close to hitting it! The beam attack was useless against a maneuvering target, but big bombers weren't expected to maneuver much.

The "sound barrier" killed a number of early test pilots. As the plane approached the speed of sound, a shock wave developed which greatly increased drag and a lot of power was needed to break through. The plane would vibrate and the shock wave would bend the flight controls, sometimes producing "control reversal" and the plane did unexpected rolls. Sweeping the wings back and stiffening the flight control surfaces (ailerons and rudder) made it possible to break the barrier. The only way for the F-86L to break the barrier was to go as high as possible, where the air was thin and resistance less, then dive straight down. I broke the sound barrier myself on Sept 8th 1958. I climbed in full afterburner to 45,000 feet, rolled over and headed straight down in full afterburner. As I dove past 35,000 feet my Mach indicator jumped past 0.98 to 1.02 and the plane rolled sharply to the left. I came out of afterburner, it rolled suddenly back to the right, and I recovered from the dive. The airplane was low on fuel after using so much afterburner, so I landed promptly. This was my first supersonic flight — later I was to reach Mach 2.0 in the F-106.

The F-86L had an electronic fuel control and an afterburner, all controlled by an analog computer. Computer control of the engine was an idea ahead of its time, as the computer wasn't reliable enough. Computer malfunctions could cause the F-86L to explode!

Instead of the pilot controlling the fuel to the engine, the pilot only selected how much power he wanted and the computer decided how much fuel to input. If the engine was going too slowly, it would add more fuel. There was also an afterburner, which is basically a ramjet located aft of the main engine and burns a lot of fuel to produce more thrust for short periods. The afterburner had exit nozzles, which were normally closed but opened when the afterburner was lit, to allow the increased volume of jet blast to exit. The pilot had a small gauge in the cockpit which told him if the engine nozzles were open or closed.

The F-86L had a swept wing, in contrast to the T-33's straight wing. The straight wing was better at slower speeds, while the swept wing allowed the F-86 to fly closer to the speed of sound before hitting the sound barrier. It could go supersonic in a steep dive. USAF Photo

Sometimes the plane would be flying in afterburner, with the nozzles open, and the computer would decide to close them. When the nozzles closed, the jet exhaust couldn't get out fast enough and the pressure in the tailpipe would increase rapidly. Increasing tailpipe pressure would slow the main jet engine. The computer would notice that the engine RPM was slower than desired, so it would add more fuel to the engine. Adding more fuel increased the pressure in the tailpipe, so the engine would slow some more. The computer would see that the engine was slowing, so it would add more fuel, repeating the cycle. It usually took about four or five seconds from the time the nozzles closed until the airplane blew up! Enough planes blew up so we had a song: *"Tra la la Boomdiay. Did you go BOOM today? Two went BOOM yesterday! Tra la la Boomdiay".*

One F-86L was taking off from Tyndall AFB in Florida when there was a sudden change in the engine power. The pilot glanced at the little nozzle gauge, and noted that the afterburner nozzles were CLOSED while the engine was in full afterburner! Just as the problem registered in his mind, there was a terrific explosion. He found himself flying through the air, in his seat, but there was no airplane! He did not eject — the plane just exploded and he was one of the pieces. He unbuckled his seat belt, pushed away from the ejection seat, and pulled his ripcord to open his parachute. He came down in the bay, uninjured, and was picked up by a fisherman.

We were changing Base Commanders at Moody AFB. The ceremony involved a parade and "Pass In Review" ceremony, with a fly-over of about twelve F-86L's in formation. As the highlight of the Change of Command ceremony, the outgoing Commander turned to the new Commander, saluted and said: "Sir, I present the Command". The new Commander returned the salute and said: "Sir, I accept the Command". Minutes later, two of the flyby aircraft had a mid-air collision and the pilots bailed out. In accordance with regulations, the new Commander was called to HQ USAF in Washington the next day to explain why he had lost two aircraft! The Commander is always responsible for whatever his troops do.

November 22, 1958. I married my college girlfriend, Midge Canty, in Auburndale, Mass.. She was a cute redhead who attracted my attention because she was vivacious and went on camping and hiking trips with our college Mountain Club. She really needed her spirit of adventure when she married me! We got married when I was on my way from Advanced Interceptor Training at Moody AFB in Florida to my first operational fighter squadron at Geiger AFB, Spokane, Washington. After the wedding reception we headed west, visiting my parents in Mendon, New York (near Rochester) and pushing on west. We stopped for the traditional honeymoon photographs at Niagara Falls, past Chicago, and into the open West. The temperature dropped as we drove through the Badlands of South Dakota, and we were almost the only visitors in the snow at Mount Rushmore. The car heater didn't work, a wheel bearing failed, and the universal joint broke. We fed starving deer in the snows of Yellowstone Park and in late December 1958 slid down the icy Idaho roads into Spokane, Washington. Our new lives together had begun, and have lasted for 57 years!

Fighter Pilot

Geiger Field, Spokane, Washington

I reported for duty with the 498th Fighter Interceptor Squadron in December 1958 to fly the F-102. It was bigger and more powerful than the F-86 and had guided missiles instead of unguided rockets, making it effective against maneuvering targets. From Spokane we defended the northwest USA, often flying north into Canada to intercept US bombers which were "penetrating" during exercises. The US bombers had good electronic countermeasures (ECM) and we learned various ways to get through their jamming. It took a lot of practice. I also flew the T-33 trainer, serving as target during exercises.

One February day I was flying a T-33 north of Spokane over the Canadian Rocky Mountains at about 40,000 feet, enjoying the beautiful mountains and the great expanse of snow underneath us, unbroken by any human habitation. Two F-102's were starting to attack me from about eighty miles away, when suddenly my engine quit! One moment the plane was humming along smoothly, warm and happy, and the next moment there was silence as warning lights blinked and the engine instruments headed toward zero! My radio transmitter lost electrical power and would not transmit my "MAYDAY" call. The plane started down in a long glide toward the snow covered mountains. My radio receiver still worked, and I could hear the F-102's reporting that the target was descending. Yes, I was descending — toward those cold mountains! The cockpit heater runs off the engine, and now the cockpit got very cold. The fighters thought I was just taking evasive action, and made a pass at me as I glided down. The mountains seemed to get bigger as I got closer — there was no place to land — I might have to bail out and survive in the Canadian Rockies for days before help could come for me! I knew the checklist said not to start the plane above 25,000 feet, but the mountains were nearly that high and my heart was in my throat. Maybe the plane would start at 30,000 feet! Ice had probably blocked the normal fuel control, so I switched to Emergency Fuel and hit the ignition. To my joy, the jet engine started — but the tailpipe temperature rapidly climbed from near zero to a thousand degrees! That was hot enough to melt parts of the tailpipe, but it gradually returned to normal. I was flying again! I was sweating from a few moments of panic. There is a saying: "Flying is hours and hours of boredom, punctuated by moments of stark terror"! As I returned to base and landed, I realized that I had nearly lost the airplane because I had started it above 25,000 feet, and the emergency fuel control is not adapted to high altitude. I learned that I needed to know a lot more about my airplanes so that I could handle them in emergencies, and not panic. A frightening lesson, but I learned well. Five years later a T-33 engine quit on me again, and I glided down to 25,000 feet before starting the engine. My passenger, a Colonel, was amazed at my delay in attempting a restart!

On another mission in the T-33, I flew down to McClellan AFB in California. It was a long flight, and I was running low on fuel. A heavy California smog was moving in, and visibility was going down rapidly. I found the radio navigation beacon and started down, noticing a strange behavior in my heading indicator. As I started to make a final turn toward base, my heading indicator failed completely. All I had for heading was an ancient magnetic compass bobbling around in a glass filled with alcohol — no better than the compasses that some people have in cars. I descended into the smog, and couldn't see anything. I went down to my minimum altitude, and still couldn't see the ground. The radio crackled with people asking me where I was — and I didn't know where I was! I took a heading from my old compass and quickly evaluated my situation. I didn't have enough fuel to get to another base — I had to land right away, or bail out! I remembered that one of my instruments — an Instrument Landing System (ILS)—used the heading indicator inputs, but also used a radio signal. It had nothing pointing toward the station, but I could dial in a radial and follow that radial to the field. As I got close, a glide slope appeared and I followed the radial and the glide slope to the field, landing in very bad smog. The smog was so bad that the plane behind me crashed and the pilot was killed. I was happy to have cheated death again, and I had learned another lesson about how to think out my problems logically and not to panic.

The 498th Fighter Interceptor Squadron was transitioning to the F-106, and the new plane was down for maintenance so often that they could not support enough flying time for our squadron pilots. The answer was to cut down the number of pilots in the squadron. I was involuntarialy transferred to the Base Personnel Office and out of fighters, although I could still fly the T-33. I learned a lot as a Personnel Officer, first being assigned to contract law violations and then to Courts Martial for several offenses.

The F-102 was much larger and more effective than the F-86D/L. It was the most advanced interceptor of its day. It could go supersonic in level flight and carried six guided missiles (three infrared and three radar) plus 24 Mighty Mouse rockets, all in an internal missile bay. After 1962, the F-102 could carry a nuclear guided missile. The delta wing was full of fuel, so it had excellent range and was highly maneuverable. Its radar was the most advanced of its time, with an effective range of 15 miles. Its radar had excellent electronic counter-countermeasures (ECCM) which could penetrate the electronic countermeasures (ECM) that new bombers carried. This is the model I flew in 1960 at Geiger Field. Later, an infrared sight was added - it was a glass bump in front of the cockpit that we called the "gumball machine". Photo from Flickr with no copyright.

A Hero—or a Murderer?

A young airman was brought in for administrative action. His various commanders had found him useless, and kept transferring him to different do-nothing jobs. His current commander wanted to discharge him from the Air Force as "unsuitable for military service". He was entitled to legal counsel, so we assigned a young Lieutenant fresh from law school as his defense counsel. We held a hearing, and the Lieutenant pointed out that none of the previous commanders had kept the airman at one job the minimum time stated in Air Force Regulations to give him a fair chance to learn the job. If we discharged the airman as "unsuitable", we were violating Air Force Regulations. We decided to give the airman another chance, assigned him to a new commander, and waited to see what would happen. We weren't ready for what happened next!

Geiger Field (now Spokane International Airport) is on one side of the Spokane River and the city of Spokane is on the other side. Very early one morning, one of our young air policemen, who lived in town, put on his uniform, strapped on his pistol, and started driving to work while listening to the police radio. A report came of an armed robbery in progress. An armed robber had held up a store and was fleeing by car with police in pursuit. The car was headed for the bridge across the river, just as our young air policeman was approaching from the other direction. Thinking quickly, our air policeman turned his car broadside on the bridge, blocking the bridge exit. The robber drove onto the bridge and couldn't get off, as the city policemen were right behind him. The robber jumped out of his car and exchanged gunfire with the city policemen. Our Air Force air policeman pulled out his trusty Air Force issue .45 automatic, took careful aim, and killed the robber with one shot!

In a few minutes there was a crowd of policemen, reporters, and Air Force officers on the bridge. The dead robber turned out to be our own airman who we were giving another chance to do better! Everyone was congratulating the air policeman for coming to the aid of the city police who were being shot at. The Base Commander said our air policeman should be awarded a medal for heroism. Then our young lawyer Lieutenant arrived on the scene.

"Did the city police request your help?" he asked. No, they hadn't.

"Did you know this was an Air Force airman that you were shooting at?" No, it was an unknown armed robber.

"Were you on duty, or were you directed by your Air Police officers to take action?" No, just driving to work. "So, entirely on your own, without any request from the civil police for help, you shot this man in the back and killed him?"

At that moment, the Commander told the young lawyer to stop asking questions in front of reporters! Instead of being a hero, our air policeman might be charged with manslaughter! Everyone hushed up the incident and I didn't hear if the air policeman was charged, but the story of our "unsuitable" airman was only half over.

We went into the dead airman's room to ship his belongings home. His room was full of stolen goods; he was an active thief. We packed up what belonged to him and shipped the stuff to his father—who was in Communist Cuba! When the hospital autopsy was over, we shipped the airman's body, with an American flag (as is customary for someone who dies on duty) to the father in Cuba. The father angrily sent back the American flag with a letter saying that, not only had we murdered his son, but an autopsy in Cuba showed that some body parts were missing — and provided us with a list of missing body parts.

Our Commander called the lawyer Lieutenant on the carpet. "If it wasn't for you, this man would have been discharged a month ago. Here is a list of body parts that the autopsy apparently removed and did not replace. GO TO THE HOSPITAL, GET THE NECESSARY PARTS, AND SHIP THEM TO CUBA!" The lawyer Lieutenant (who was a good friend of mine) had to go to the hospital and get parts from cadavers with the right blood type and ship them off to Cuba.

Design Deficiencies Kill

For the first few years, the F-106's advanced radar and computer were all based on vacuum-tube technology, and were unreliable. Our radio was supposed to be much more powerful than the F-102 radio, but it failed so often that we always flew two F-106's together so one could lead if the other had radio failure. We sent up two planes and they both had radio failure!

The F-106's engine was powerful but had reliability problems. One of my Squadron friends took up an F-106 and had engine failure when one of the compressor blades in his engine broke and went back into the engine, causing progressive failure. My friend tried to get the airplane back to base, but had to eject a few miles from home. He was low; his parachute did not fully open and he was killed as he hit the ground. I was put on the accident board and saw the photos of my dead friend, facedown in a field connected to his half-opened parachute. We focused on the engine failure, but we should have paid more attention to the failure of the parachute system.

Parachute design in the early 1960's concentrated on high-speed bailouts. Jet aircraft went so fast that a human would be killed by the wind blast if he ejected at high speed. The F-106 had a complex ejection system which would save a pilot during a high-speed ejection in level flight. The trouble was that most ejections occur at low altitudes and low speeds, when the pilot is "out of altitude, airspeed, and ideas".

F-106 pilots wore "spurs", clamps on the heels of our boots. When we climbed into the cockpit, we hooked the "spurs" to cables on the base of the ejection seat. When the pilot pulled the ejection handle, a series of 44 events occurred to achieve the ejection. First, a small charge tightened the cables and pulled the pilot's feet back tightly against the seat (preventing them from flailing in the wind). The canopy blew off, panels rose on both sides of the pilot and the floor curled up in a protective pan around the feet that were tight against the seat. The ejection seat quickly rose up on rails, then rotated backwards. For an instant, the pilot was lying on his back with his feet pointed forward, protected from the windblast by the seat pan. Then a rocket fired, and the seat went forward and up high enough to get over the tail of the aircraft which might hit him from behind. The parachute then deployed from the seat, bringing the pilot, seat, and survival equipment together safely to the ground.

The next bailout was at a different squadron. The pilot pulled the ejection handles, the foot cables retracted, the canopy blew, the seat rose up the rails and onto the back of the airplane — but the rocket motor did not fire! The pilot was now lying on his back, feet forward, securely strapped into an ejection seat that would not leave the airplane. He died in that position when the plane hit the ground.

Then, near Boston, a pilot had engine failure and tried to eject. The cables pulled his feet back to the seat, the side panels came up, the canopy ejected, and then everything stopped. The pilot's feet were securely held to the seat, but the seat did not go up the rails. The pilot could not get out of the airplane so he grabbed the stick again and brought the plane in for a crash landing. The plane caught fire but did not explode. He was close enough to the base that the rescue ambulance drove over the field to find the pilot half out of the cockpit, sitting on the canopy rail of the burning airplane, with one foot still in the cockpit. The pilot had got one "spur" off of the cable, but the other "spur" was still attached and he could not get free. The medic helped get the pilot's boot off. They left the boot in the burning airplane and got away. In the report that I read, it said that *"The pilot's jaw was broken in the crash. His jaw was wired shut, so he was unable to make a statement to the investigators"*. I can guess what he would have said! We switched to a more conventional seat with better low-altitude capability.

I was then reassigned to fly F-102's in Alaska.

Alaska—and the Spirit of Attack

In July 1961 Midge, baby Julie and I drove up the Alaska Highway, where I joined the 317th Fighter Interceptor Squadron flying F-102's. Flying in Alaska was a wonderful experience, and I became an excellent pilot. We flew from outlying bases: King Salmon on the Aleutian Peninsula, Galena in the western part of Alaska, and Eielson AFB, 25 miles from Fairbanks. We flew against very difficult "targets" — our own pilots flying B-57 light bombers or T-33 trainers. They frequently flew extremely low or made sharp turns to get away from us. I learned even more about radar, so that I could get the best performance from radar and infrared even when the target used jamming (ECM). I pulled Alert duty in the Alert Hangar, fully armed and waiting for the Russians to come. We were usually on Alert for about 60 hours per week (compared to 40-hour weeks for civilians). It was the most critical part of the Cold War, and Russian bombers frequently tested our defenses. I had at least twelve "Active Air" scrambles against unknown aircraft, some of which were Russian. The Russians knew international law, and usually stayed outside the 20-mile limit of American territory. They would probe our defenses to show that they could (and to record our radar site locations). We would intercept them to prove that, in real war, we could shoot them down. Our son Brian was born at Elmendorf AFB in January 1962; the Cuban Crisis was in October 1962, and in March 1964 we went through the Great Alaska Earthquake.

"ONLY THE SPIRIT OF ATTACK BORNE IN A BRAVE HEART WILL BRING SUCCESS TO ANY FIGHTER AIRCRAFT, NO MATTER HOW HIGHLY DEVELOPED THE AIRCRAFT MAY BE". The squadron motto hung over our door, and soon I found how true it was. Alaskan airspace was largely free of the air traffic control regulations which controlled us in the "Lower 48" States. We flew in weather which would horrify today's safety officers. Our targets flew so low in between the banks of rivers that they left a wake in the water. Our targets would turn aggressively into us. I would be attacking a "high altitude" target and find that it had dived to low altitude and was far below me. Once I flew against a low altitude target and was surprised to see him leaving a contrail at least 20,000 feet above where he was supposed to be! After a few lessons in humility, my fangs began to grow and I got AGGRESSIVE. I was attacking, and my target could not get away!

One day we had a "Sky Shield" exercise, and our own B-52 bombers from Strategic Air Command attacked Alaska. Bombers came from over the Arctic Ocean and up from the Aleutian Islands. They jammed our radar, and they jammed the ground search radar. I homed in on their jamming signals and always got my target. On another day, a real Russian plane came at low altitude and flew just over the arctic ice pack. He was more than three miles out to sea, so we didn't shoot. He twisted and turned, but I got onto him and took photos. I felt good; I had found and photographed my first real Russian plane. When I looked at the other planes in the sky, I knew that they flew by because I allowed them to fly by. I was a FIGHTER PILOT, and the sky belonged to ME!

Cuban Missile Crisis—seen from Alaska

October 1962 has gone down in history as the most critical time of the Cold War — we came closer to nuclear war with the Soviet Union (i.e., the Russians) than at any other time. The Russians were building intercontinental ballistic missiles (ICBMs) with nuclear warheads to target the USA, but their missiles weren't very reliable. They had some good,

The Spirit of Attack

reliable intermediate range ballistic missiles (IRBMs) with nuclear warheads, but they didn't have the range to hit America. They gave the Cuban Communist dictator, Fidel Castro, plenty of weapons — with which he was able to beat the inept Bay of Pigs attack that our Central Intelligence Agency (CIA) launched against Castro early in the Kennedy administration.

The Soviet leader, Nikita Khruschev, met our President Kennedy for a summit meeting. Khruschev decided that Kennedy was soft and could be pushed around. The Soviets then sent missiles and nuclear warheads to Cuba. Once in place in Cuba, the missiles would be threaten most of the USA, and could possibly wipe out our bombers on the ground. Nuclear missiles in Cuba would tip the balance of power in Russia's favor.

One of our U-2 high-altitude spy planes flew over Cuba and got photographs of the Russians unloading missiles and nuclear weapons. The entire existence of the USA would be threatened if the missiles could be assembled and loaded with their nuclear warheads. More Russian missiles were on ships headed for Cuba. President Kennedy said that the Russian ships would not be allowed to get to Cuba. The Russians replied that the ships had the freedom of the seas, and that they would not stop their ships. The US forces went on full combat alert as the Russian ships continued to sail toward the American naval blockade. The Russians continued to assemble their missiles in Cuba, readying them for launch against the USA.

The Russians said that our blockade was an act of war, and said that their intercontinental missiles in Russia would destroy us. We did not have many ICBMs, but President Kennedy knew that the Russian ICBMs were unreliable. Our Strategic Air Command (SAC) bombers were very reliable. The US built up forces in Florida in preparation for an invasion of Cuba. The Russian missiles were not ready to fire, so Kennedy continued the blockade. The Cubans then shot down one of our U-2 spy planes which was trying to get current photos of the missiles in Cuba; our pilot was killed. Fidel Castro of Cuba wanted war with the USA, and made strong statements on the radio. Nuclear war seemed very likely as the Russian ships kept coming toward our naval blockade — then the Russian ships slowed down, and finally stopped a few miles short of our ships. The Russians realized that they were not strong enough to win a war, and finally agreed to remove their missiles and nuclear warheads from Cuba in return for a US pledge never to invade Cuba.

In Alaska, my day started normally as I drove to the Alert Hangar at Elmendorf AFB near Anchorage. I listened to the morning news, which said that something strange was going on in Washington and that President Kennedy was meeting with members of the National Security Council. I arrived at the Alert Hangar, put my parachute and helmet in my F-102, and took over duty as Alert Force Commander with four fighters. The Command Center phoned me to say that we were bringing all our 18 fighters up on highest alert, and that we were having a "practice" loading of nuclear weapons on our fighters. An hour later we had a briefing from three Generals telling us of the Cuban crisis — Generals had never visited us before — they suddenly realized that it was the lowly fighter pilots who would actually fight the war!

My four fighters were promptly deployed north to Eielson AFB near Fairbanks, carrying nuclear weapons, and were ready for war at any time. I set up on Alert in Eielson and watched intelligence reports as the Russian ships got closer to our naval blockade. Eielson was a beehive of activity, with bombers, tankers, and U-2 spy planes taking off at all hours of the day or night. We did not know if we would ever see our families again. The Air Force had a plan to evacuate all dependents from Anchorage to Seward, Alaska. The wives would have to get there by themselves — they kept their autos filled with gas and carried a case of "C" rations (and gas masks) in the cars. There was no doubt about it — we were ready for war!

Our bombers began to "push" the Russians, flying right toward Russia and turning back at the last moment. The Russians could see the bombers on their radar, and knew that a word from President Kennedy would send our bombers deep into Russia, bringing nuclear devastation. Russian fighters were strong in only a few places and their intercontinental missiles were unreliable. Their bombers lacked the aerial refueling tankers that our bombers routinely used, so the number that could reach us was limited. We were ready for their bombers to try something. I was scrambled twice against unknown aircraft: once it was a civilian airliner coming in from Europe, and once it was one of our own B-52 bombers which made a navigation error while coming back from the Russian border and was not where he should have been.

We "pushed" the Russians, and they did not push back. They apparently did not have as much military power as they claimed. One of our spies, Colonel Penkovsky of Russian intelligence, told us that their intercontinental nuclear missiles were not ready and could not be fired. We were "eyeball to eyeball" and they backed off. Gradually the crisis eased, as President Kennedy made an agreement with the Russian leader, Nikita Khruschev, which required the Russians to remove the missiles in return for our promise not to invade Cuba. The worst crisis of the Cold War came to an end, and we never gain came so close to war.

Wingman Bailout

"C" Flight in Alaska, 1964. I am second from left in the front row. Dean Rands, whose "Wingman Bailout" story is on this page, is in the front row on the right. Dean was flying the F-102 by Mount McKinley on the last page of this book, a beautiful photo of the harsh beauty of Alaska in winter.

A fighter squadron is a true "band of brothers" bonded by training and experiences. We knew we could count on each other when our lives were in danger.

As the Cuban Crisis ended, I took off from Eielson AFB (Fairbanks) with my wingman, Dean Rands. We were to fly some practice intercepts and then land back home at Elmendorf (Anchorage). After we'd been airborne for a half hour, he reported an "Oil Pressure Low" warning light and engine vibrations. I joined in loose formation with him and tried to find a place for him to land. There was a wide area of clouds which obscured our view of the ground, but the ceiling under the clouds was pretty good. We declared an emergency, and the radar controller gave us a vector to an airfield with 8,400 feet of hard surface runway. I was very pleased, as that's a good runway for fighters — but I couldn't think of any airfield in the area with that good a runway. "Any port in a storm" as they say, so we headed our fighters toward this unexpectedly good piece of concrete. As we got close to it, the radar controller suddenly apologized for his mistake — it was 4,800 feet of gravel — he had read the map wrong! There was no way that Dean could land on 4,800 feet of gravel, and his engine was vibrating violently.

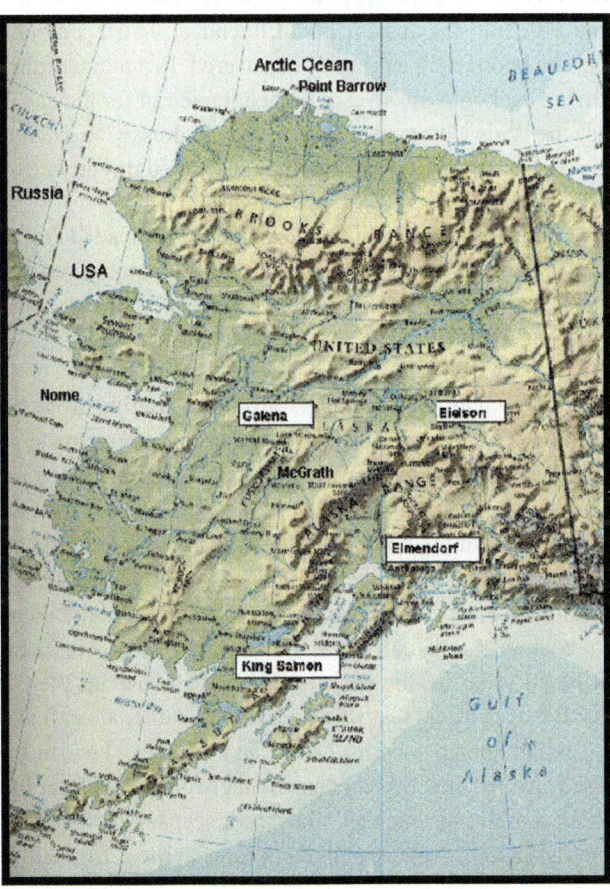

We descended until we were just over the undercast of clouds; it was time to bail out. Dean made his last radio call and I watched the canopy blow off, followed by Dean in his ejection seat. I barely saw his parachute open as he and his plane descended into the thick layer of clouds. I was afraid of running into either Dean in his parachute or his pilotless plane in the clouds, so I swung wide and started down through the clouds. My memory of Alaskan terrain told me that there were no big mountains in the area, but I was violating all sorts of regulations to descend into clouds without proper clearance or knowing what the terrain and weather were really like. I was not going to let my friend down, and I was going to take whatever risks were needed to help him. I got under the clouds in time to see a ball of fire on a ridge not far away. I flew over to Dean's wrecked plane, but could not find his parachute. I was running low on fuel, so I had to fly back to Elmendorf alone.

By the time I got back to Elmendorf, a rescue mission was already under way. The Squadron immediately thought of Dean's wife, Bev, who was pregnant. They were afraid that Bev would hear of the accident on the radio or television, so they called Bev's best friend and told her to go to visit with Bev and keep her busy and not let her turn on the radio or TV. Bev's friend complied immediately, scooping up a small child and going over for a surprise visit. The friend stayed and stayed, as the hours ticked away. Bev began to get suspicious that something was up.

Meanwhile, Dean had landed by parachute in Alaskan scrub pine forest. He saw my plane flying near the smoke of his plane, but I was pretty far away from him. It would get dark soon, so Dean wisely decided to make camp and wait for morning. He opened his survival kit, got out his sleeping bag, etc., and turned on the emergency "beeper" radio homing signal. He hung the radio in a tree and proceeded to make camp. He was a long way from our closest helicopter, at Galena Air Base on the Yukon River. The rescue helicopter had scrambled even before Dean had bailed out, picked up the beeper and homed in on it. Dean had started a fire and was about to make supper when the helicopter came right to his campsite and lowered a sling to pick him up!

As soon as Dean was safely aboard the helicopter, it radioed the good news back to Elmendorf. The Squadron Commander had assembled the usual next-of-kin notification team: himself plus a doctor (because Bev was pregnant), a Chaplain, and a Finance Officer (who gives an immediate lump of money to a widow so she doesn't have a financial crisis in the first few days). The team knew that Dean was safe, so they piled into a staff car and headed for Bev's apartment. Bev was already suspicious that her best friend was overstaying her welcome, and was washing dishes when she looked through the kitchen window and saw the notification team arrive. She screamed and cried as the Squadron Commander came through the door exclaiming "HE IS OK! HE'S OK!"

Russian Bombers Over Alaska

One day we had a big exercise and downloaded the missiles from most of our aircraft so we could use them for training against American bombers that simulated an attack on us. It was a hard day of flying, and late that evening I finally got back to our base housing apartment at Elmendorf. I stripped out of my winter flightsuit and climbed into the tub for a relaxing bath. The phone rang, and Midge answered. In a moment she called out: "The Squadron wants you back IMMEDIATELY!" I hurried back into my sweaty flightsuit and ran for the car. When I entered the Squadron Operations Office, I was startled to see the Wing Commander giving orders, dressed in a bathrobe and slippers! "Russian bombers have penetrated 200 miles into Alaska, near McGrath, and they're headed directly for Anchorage"!

I grabbed my parachute and helmet and headed for my aircraft. I had no missiles because our fighters had been downloaded for the exercise. In a couple of minutes a convoy of weapons vehicles came and we loaded the missiles in record time (ignoring some safety directives). In another few minutes I was airborne from Anchorage, heading directly for the Russian bombers.

We now had twelve fighters airborne, coming from bases in Galena, Fairbanks (Eielson AFB), King Salmon, and Anchorage (Elmendorf AFB). Our radar controllers made a major error: all fighters were directed to cut off the Russians before they reached Anchorage, but none were positioned for a change of direction. The Russians suddenly turned around and headed back to Russia as fast as they could go, and we were all badly positioned, in a stern chase! Our F-102's were not much faster than the bombers. The bombers scooted west as fast as they could go — they knew they had fighters coming for them, and radioed for help from Russia. Russian fighters took off from Provodinia air base in Siberia and headed east to protect their bombers. We caught up with the Russian bombers just as they crossed the International Date Line, which put them back in Russian airspace. There were twelve American fighters and two Russian bombers headed west, and a bunch of Russian MIGs heading east — everyone turned off their lights — the radar screen was full of aircraft in a disorganized mess. We were afraid that we would run into other aircraft in the dark, and we were in Russian airspace at that moment—and the Russian fighters were in American airspace! The Command Post radioed for us to return home. Nobody saw anything or fired any missiles. We concluded that two Russian Bear bombers had been on a navigation mission, but the frozen tundra of Alaska might have looked like Arctic icepack on their radar. They apparently were lost, and didn't know that they were over Alaska until American fighters came at them from all directions.

Unidentified Flying Objects (UFOs)

Early one winter night I was scrambled from King Salmon air base on the Aleutian peninsula and directed north to the small airfield at McGrath. The tower operator at McGrath reported that a UFO was circling his airport. We couldn't find a UFO, but the planet Venus was unusually bright . . .

Hunting in Alaska was a real experience. Here I am with a near-record Dall Sheep ram that I shot in the Wrangell Mountains about 300 miles northeast of Anchorage.

A few months later I was flying my F-102 after one of our "target" aircraft, a T-33 which was flying very low along the Yukon River. As I flew low over the river and prepared to attack, I looked up and saw a bright star above me. It was mid-afternoon — there shouldn't be any stars at all — what was that thing? I broke off my attack on the T-33 and climbed rapidly, reporting that I was going after an <u>unidentified flying object!</u> The Command Post got excited, and kept asking for reports.

I climbed to 40,000 feet, as high as the F-102 could go, and the object was still many thousands of feet above me. Now I could see that it was a balloon with a gondola hanging under it. As I watched, the balloon popped — a big strip of material tore off and the balloon began to fall. A few moments later, the gondola detached from the balloon and fell by itself. A small parachute popped out from the gondola to stabilize it — then a larger parachute opened — and it was still far above me! The Command Post could hardly believe my running narrative of what was happening. I was running low on fuel and had to leave, but the Command Post had diverted a C-130 transport plane into my area. The C-130 could see the gondola and parachute as I turned south for home, low on fuel.

The C-130 transport had plenty of fuel, and circled while the gondola descended. The Command Post contacted the Army at Fairbanks, who sent helicopters to pick up the gondola. They discovered that the balloon had been launched from France, many thousands of miles away!

Another UFO incident occurred in the spring of 1963. A slow ship was being tracked by our radar — we thought it might be a Russian ice breaker, coming too close to American territory. Nobody was too excited until the "ship" crossed the shoreline and came inland! The Command Post scrambled fighters, who reported that the "ship" was a large balloon with a gondola, drifting across Alaska at low altitude. We wanted to get a look at the gondola, but didn't have any planes with machine guns to shoot down the balloon — and our missiles would probably home in on the gondola, destroying the very thing that we wanted to look at. A sergeant's suggestion was taken up immediately: we took a small anchor from a fishing boat, sharpened the flukes, and attached it to a target tow reel that we had on a T-33 trainer. The T-33 flew out to the balloon, reeled out the anchor on the thin tow wire, flew low over the balloon and snagged it with the anchor, popping the balloon. The tow wire snapped immediately and the gondola fell into the tundra, where a helicopter picked it up. I never heard where the balloon had come from.

Military Exercises

Our "Spirit of Attack" grew as our F-102's were sent against some very difficult targets in exercises. The most common target was the T-33 trainer, and later B-57 light bombers with Electronic Countermeasures (ECM) became frequent targets. At one time, we had F-102s, T-33s, and B-57s all in the 317th Fighter Interceptor Squadron. We may have been the only fighter squadron with bombers assigned. On special exercises called "Sky Shield", our Strategic Air Command (SAC) sent B-52 bombers against us. The B-52 had plenty of ECM but they were so big that I never had much trouble finding and "killing" the B-52s. They seldom did any serious maneuvers which could have thrown us off the track.

The T-33s and B-57s were flown by pilots who knew us very well and knew that our greatest weakness was knowing the altitude of the target. The radar sites would often get an early reading on the target from their height finder, and not check it again when they concentrated on vectoring the interceptors onto the target. The T-33s and B-57s would listen to our radio calls, and would pick a critical moment to make major changes in altitude and direction. While the B-52s were limited by their own rules to only about a 500 ft/minute climb or descent and a 10 degree heading change, the T-33s and B-57s would suddenly descend at 1,500 or even 2,000 ft/minute and change heading by more than 45 degrees. Sometimes they'd even turn in a tight circle, completely confusing the radar controllers who were trying to plot a course on the target. While the radar controller was trying to figure out what the target was doing, the targets would be changing altitude and the controller wouldn't get a new reading. As a result, when our fighters

The TU-95 Bear was the Soviet Union's primary long-range bomber. It was fast with double contra-rotating turboprop propellers, had in-flight refueling (see the probe in the nose) and defensive guns. Note the tail turret
USAF Photo.

came in at perhaps 35,000' looking for the target, the target might be down at almost ground level, scooting across the Alaskan tundra. Our radar generally searched level with our fighters, so our fighter at 35,000 feet could search from 45,000 feet down to 25,000 feet, and not see a target that was low. On the other hand, a target that was supposed to be low might climb as rapidly as he could. We would be at 500 feet, looking for a low target, and the target might be at 20,000 feet and climbing!

The B-57 had better high-altitude performance than the F-102. On one high altitude attack, I made a head-on attack and got my B-57 OK, and swung around in a tight turn to make a second, tail attack with infrared missiles. A good plan, but the B-57 turned hard and was just above me when I saw what he was doing. I needed to get some distance from him so I could fire my missiles (simulated, of course) but when I slowed down to let him get ahead, he slowed down, too. I turned to one side to get some lateral distance from him, but he turned and stayed just above me. Damn, I was frustrated! I could see him clearly, always a thousand feet directly above me, and I could not get behind him! I finally gave up and went home — the B-57 had defeated me.

The T-33s had very good low-speed, low-altitude performance and could turn on a dime. Going after a T-33 at low altitude in Alaska was a real challenge, as the pilots knew us personally and could be awfully tricky. T-33s would fly down the Yukon River so low that they'd be inside the river banks. Our radar was not effective if we were above a target that was flying low; the ground clutter was too bad unless we flew lower than the target and could spotlight him against the sky. I was once chasing a low T-33 and was flying so low myself that a grizzly bear reared up on its hind legs to take a swipe at me! On another occasion I was chasing a low T-33 and was "bounced" by a second T-33 which dropped down on my tail from above. The "Spirit of Attack" grew every day; I went after the targets with my eyes wide open, my radar searching high and low, trying infrared to find low targets, and swearing to myself that the targets would not get past me!

Years later I flew in Michigan against many targets, but none were as hard as the Alaskan targets. We flew at 50 feet in Alaska but 500 feet in Michigan, to reduce noise to people on the ground. Once in Michigan I decided to make it harder for the F-106 that was attacking me. Instead of holding the 250 knots airspeed that we always used, I pushed my speed up to

350 knots. The fighter pilot behind me never understood what was wrong, and the radar controller never told him that I was going fast. I even gave them a hint, by calling out: *"Run, Run, as fast as you can, you can't catch me, I'm the Gingerbread Man!"* I went all the way across Michigan without the F-106 catching me. His plane was plenty fast enough — it could go 650 knots if needed — but the pilot simply didn't have the "Spirit of Attack".

Icy Runways

Breaking action on a runway is measured by driving a car down the runway and slamming on the brakes. A decelerometer is strapped into the car, and measures how quickly the car stops. Multiple stops along the runway are averaged together. A dry runway was about 24. Good braking action was above 15, and we would fly until it got down to 5. By the time I retired from the Air Force (in 1968), the Air Force had become so cautious that wouldn't let us fly if the braking action was less than 15. One winter day I was coming back to Elmendorf from a week on Alert in Galena, and there was ice on the runway at Elmendorf. Average braking action was 5, but "Watch the turn-off point—it's really slick". I slowed down my F-102 and made a nice landing, using my drag chute to slow me down properly. All was under control as I came to the turn-off point, and tapped the brakes gently. The F-102 smoothly slid around until I was going BACKWARDS down the runway! I added a bit of engine power, came to a stop, then moved back up the runway to my turnoff point and got off the runway. Then I called for a tow truck and shut down the engine—I wasn't going to try to taxi in with that much ice! On another occasion, I watched one of my friends going backwards down the runway at Galena. He agreed that it was a memorable experience!

Alaskan Cold

Elmendorf AFB and Anchorage were protected from real cold by the Alaska Range of mountains, including Mt. McKinley. North of the Alaska Range is a large low area. It is marshy and hard to move across in summer. In winter, cold air stagnates and just gets colder. Eielson and Galena were our two bases in this cold zone. Eielson AFB was near the large city of Fairbanks, and a 1947 Ford military staff car was provided for the pilots' use when off duty. This car was 16 years old and should have been in a museum. It had a gasoline-powered heater! When you turned on the heater, you could hear the fire roar to life and the heat was immediate and hot! I thought it might blow up or something, so I was afraid to use it. Most cars in Alaska had headbolt heaters, dipstick heaters, or water circulating heaters. Parking spots had electrical outlets on posts, so you plugged your car's heater into the power outlet whenever you parked. All the cars with wires running to posts looked like an old cavalry picture with the horses tied up outside the saloon. The heaters made it easier to start your car in the cold, but there were other problems. Sometimes the grease in the wheel bearings would freeze and the wheels wouldn't turn. The rear wheels would turn because the engine was driving them, but sometimes you'd move along with one or both of your front wheels not turning and you couldn't steer. When the wheels did turn, the place where the tires had rested on the ground was a flat spot frozen onto the tire. We called it "square tires" as we bumped along until the pounding warmed the tires and they got round again.

I attended Arctic Survival School at Eielson AFB. They sent us out into the wilderness with just the parachutes and survival kits that pilots would have if they bailed out. We dug snow caves or made teepees out of parachutes. The rule was that we would be brought back for safety reasons if the temperature dropped below minus30 degrees F., but it was a balmy minus 20 when I was out there camping. They told us to take off our boots, socks, and flight suits before climbing into our sleeping bags. Golly, it's COLD when you stick your bare feet into a minus 20 degree sleeping bag!

We learned that minus 40 degrees F. is the point where the air cannot contain any water vapor, so the dew point is always 100%. Any added moisture immediately turns into an ice fog. A by-product of combustion is water, so any ground power unit or an airplane taxiing for takeoff can create an ice fog. One of our pilots flew to Galena on a beautiful, clear, cold day. He made a practice low approach over the runway first, then turned around to come back and land. His first approach laid a fog bank (at high altitude, we'd call it a contrail) right along the runway and closed the runway due to low visibility. He had to fly to an alternate field to land!

At minus fifty degrees, if you toss a glass of warm water in the air it will vaporize before the water falls back to ground. I tried it, taking a glass of hot tap water outside our Alert hangar and tossing it up. There was a big "poof" of steam; I did hear a few little ice crystals falling back on the snow. I remembered the old saying that "hot water freezes faster than cold water". I took two glasses of water, one hot, one cold, outside and watched them freeze. The cold water froze much faster than the hot water, so the old saying was wrong. The Air Police guard thought I was crazy.

Electronic Countermeasures (ECM)

I became fascinated by ECM. Barrage jamming, sweep jamming, spot jamming, angle deception, range deception, chaff, communications jamming. Everything that a bomber could use, we saw in Alaska. For everything the bomber threw at us, there was a counter-countermeasure. ECM went through an interesting cycle as bombers developed new techniques and used them against fighters, and fighters developed new methods to work through the jamming. The USAF got so good at both sides of the ECM / ECCM battle that nobody else in the world could come close to us. ECM equipment became so expensive that only American bombers could carry it and the Russians seemed to give up because of the cost. I don't think our modern fighters have as good ECCM equipment as we had in the 1970's because potential enemies have given up trying to develop ECM. We currently have a lot of ECM for jamming enemy ground radars and missiles, such as in Iraq. Our ECM and ECCM is so good that we don't have any competition anymore. The British couldn't afford modern ECM, so they flew their planes very low during the 1991 Gulf War to get below enemy missile attacks and lost too many planes. We also gave our allies ECM support. A fighter or bomber penetrating enemy airspace without ECM is a good target for enemy missiles.

"Battle Stations" and "Silent Scramble"

"BATTLE STATIONS!" The loudspeaker blared and the SCRAMBLE horn blared intermittently. We ran to our planes, started engines, and waited in the chocks for further orders. "Battle Stations" meant for the pilots to get in the cockpit, reducing scramble time by several minutes. Then the order was relayed by crewchiefs: SILENT SCRAMBLE! We taxied out and took off quickly without saying a word on the radio. We believed the Russians were listening to our radio calls so they would turn their planes around when they heard us coming. We flew to a designated spot, where we broke radio silence and got orders to descend low to the icepack. We went down and found a twin-turboprop Russian aircraft probing around our shores. He was unarmed but took evasive action when he saw us. I flew close enough to get photos of him for our intelligence guys to look at. He was probably recording the frequencies and low-altitude coverage of our air-defense radars. We do that to them all the time, so we have a "gentlemen's agreement" not to shoot anyone down. Russian bombers would "cage" their guns in a safe position so they weren't a direct threat—although the guns could still fire in a few seconds.

Kamikaze

New kinds of electronic countermeasures were being developed. We constantly improved our counter-countermeasures, added infrared tracking and advanced home-on-jam techniques. The possibility existed that the Russians might develop effective ECM which would surprise and defeat us. What would we do if we attacked, fired our radar missiles, and the Russians jammed the radar missiles? We'd fire our infrared missiles. What if they dropped flares which caused our IR missiles to miss? What do we do then?

The bomber would be carrying nuclear weapons and be headed toward your home, your loved ones, and your country. With no missiles left, you ram. Our manuals wrote about the "elevator pass" where you came up from underneath and knocked off part of the bomber's tail, causing it to lose control and crash. There was about a 50% chance that you could survive the collision and bail out later. That seemed stupid to me, because you'd be approaching at relatively slow speed and the bomber's defensive guns would shoot you down as you got in close. The worst thing would be for you to be killed without your stopping the bomber. Even if you succeeded in knocking the bomber into a fatal spin, a "dead man switch" might be activated. A "dead man switch" was a way that the bomber would arm its nuclear bomb as it crossed into enemy territory, and the bomb would then go off when the airplane fell below a certain altitude. Even if the bomber was shot down before it got to its target, the nuclear bomb would go off causing devastation and radiation somewhere in the enemy country. A "dead man switch" meant that you not only had to kill the bomber, but you had to kill the weapon, too. A nuclear bomb is filled with high explosives which are very carefully timed to all go off at the same instant. If you could hit the bomb hard enough, you would set off some of the explosives in an uncontrolled manner, causing a "single-point detonation". The high explosives would go off, but with little or no nuclear blast. It would kill you and kill the bomber crew, but you would have achieved "weapon kill" and protected your home, loved ones, and country.

The Japanese had proven in WW II that it is very hard to stop a fighter flown by a suicidal pilot. Their Kamikaze attacks had been very effective, killing thousands of Americans and sinking or damaging many ships. They had effectively used Kamikaze against our B-29 bombers over Japan. I made up my own mind that if it was necessary to stop a Russian bomber and my missiles didn't work, I would use Kamikaze. I would get ahead and above the bomber, light my afterburner and dive into the bomber at supersonic speed, aiming for the point where the wing joins the fuselage. That's where the bomb is. I would kill myself, the bomber crew, and the weapon. I believe that all of our fighter pilots had the same attitude — we would sacrifice our lives to stop the bombers. We had the "spirit of attack" in its ultimate form.

Iditarod

The Iditarod is an Alaskan sled dog race from Anchorage to Nome. It commemorates a 1925 event in which a dog sled team rushed across the tundra to deliver medicine to Nome during a diphtheria epidemic. The Iditarod came to my mind one day when I was asked to carry medicine under hazardous conditions.

An ice storm hit Elmendorf, and nothing was moving. I was in the Squadron doing some routine paperwork when the Operations Officer said there was a sick child at the Dillingham Native Hospital, and they needed the medicine badly. The weather at King Salmon was good, but the Elmendorf runway was closed by ice. Would I take the risk and try to fly the medicine to King Salmon?

I thought of the Iditarod, and of my own motto "Be Spring-Loaded in the GO Position!". Sure, I'd go. I was very well qualified in the T-33, which I had first learned to fly in Laredo, Texas and had flown again at Geiger and in Alaska. The problem was that the T-33 uses brakes for steering (there is no nosewheel steering), and with almost zero traction there would be no way to steer the plane for taxiing to the runway or on takeoff roll.

I got my parachute, helmet, etc., got the medicine box and went to my T-33. Maintenance crews had already sprayed it with an ethylene glycol de-icing fluid, and the ice around the plane was covered with a layer of mixed water and glycol. It was "slick as greased owl shit", as we said. I strapped the medicine box into the rear cockpit and made my walk-around to check the airplane. I slipped and fell down twice, soaking my flight suit with glycol and water.

The plan was to tow my airplane to the runway and start the engine when facing directly down the runway. Once the engine started, even idle thrust would cause it to start moving down the runway—brakes or chocks would not hold it! I'd have to come up to full power quickly and get going fast enough down the runway so the rudder would have directional control in the wind.

The first step—tow the airplane to the runway—failed. I sat in the cockpit and watched as the tow truck hooked up to my plane, and then the tow truck's tires just spun around on the ice without moving me an inch! We radioed for help and soon a small crowd of airmen came slipping and sliding out to the plane. They started pushing on the wings, drop tanks, and tail, and we began to move. I saw the airmen sliding and falling as they pushed. Finally we got pointed directly down the runway. A jet engine doesn't need to warm up, so I started the engine and smoothly moved the throttle up to 100% power. The plane rolled forward gathering speed and in a few seconds I had enough airspeed to control direction with my rudder; seconds later I was airborne on my way to King Salmon. It was my personal Iditarod, rushing medicine to someone in a remote part of Alaska despite the risks.

Landing Short

"There are two kinds of pilots—those who have landed short, and those who will land short". The alternative is also bad: if you land long, you may go off the far end of the runway. I was flying my F-102 to Galena, a remote Alaskan airfield on a bend in the Yukon River. The runway was slick, with ice and snow. Measured braking action was 7 (the minimum these days is usually twice that). Galena had a tricky airfield. It was short (8,600 feet instead of the usual 10,000 to 15,000 feet). They had disconnected the arresting cables because Galena was so cold that the arresting cable mechanism would freeze solid. Each year the Yukon River floods, so Galena had a 50' earthen dike on each end of its runway to keep the river out. They put red warning lights on poles on top of the dike. The far end of the runway went up a dike, so if you didn't stop on the runway you'd go up and over into the Yukon River!

I was supremely confident in my ability to fly the F-102 to the limit of its performance. *"It is my body—I am its brain"*. I could feel every throb of the engine, every burble on the wings, and could make it do exactly what I wanted. I dropped the landing gear and slowed the plane to minimum flying speed. I staggered toward the dike with a high angle of attack; aerodynamic drag would help stop me. As I passed over the dike I deployed my drag chute while still in the air (which would horrify flight safety officers). Just then I felt a slight metallic "tick" which I didn't recognize.

I landed smoothly and taxied to the Alert Hangar. A fire truck followed me. Why would a fire truck follow ME? I taxied in and shut down. The fire truck pulled up beside me and the firemen, dressed in their white firefighting suits, walked to my plane. I opened the canopy, took off my helmet and mask, and called to the firemen: "Is anything wrong?" "Yes, sir, you hit the approach lights on the dike". "Who, ME?" I asked. Then, as I climbed down the ladder . . . psssssss . . . the left tire on my plane went flat! There was a little hole in the tread.

A week after they replaced the lights, the Squadron Commander hit them! If the Commander hit the lights, they must be too high. They put the lights on shorter poles and nobody else hit them.

Murder at Galena

I was on Alert in Galena when the phone rang with the start of a remarkable series of reports from the bar at the Yukon Inn. That evening a native got into an argument with his father-in-law, pulled out a hunting knife and stabbed him. The father-in-law collapsed under the bar and the young man stormed out of the bar and across the street to his home. The barkeep looked the man over, declared him dead, and offered a round of drinks on the house in memory of the dead man. Then they had a round of drinks in sympathy with the young man who was now across the street in his home.

There were no policemen in Galena, so the State Police in Anchorage were called and everyone waited. Someone suggested that the man should have Last Rites, so they called our Base Chaplain (there were no clergy in Galena town). The Chaplain came out, examined the dead man, said some good words, and then asked: "Where is the young man who did this awful deed?" They pointed at the house across the street. The Chaplain went across the street and knocked on the door. The young man answered the door, talked to the Chaplain for a few minutes, then the Chaplain went inside the house and closed the door. The customers at the bar had a round of drinks in memory of the Chaplain.

"Is this guy really dead?" "Yeah, I looked at him. He's dead." "Are you medically trained?" "No, but I've seen a lot of dead moose, and this guy looks dead to me." "We better get a professional opinion." They called our Base Clinic and the duty nurse came out. She examined the man and pronounced him officially dead. She phoned our Base Air Police, but they wouldn't have anything to do with a murder in the native town. The nurse went back to her clinic. The bar customers had a round of drinks in honor of the officially dead man.

"This bar is pretty warm, and it might be days before a policeman can get out here from Anchorage. We can't leave the body here—he'll spoil." So they took the body out to the meat locker and laid him out with the moose meat. A policeman flew out from Anchorage the next day, heard the story, went across the street and knocked on the door. The Chaplain came out with the young man, who had agreed to give himself up. We in the Alert Hangar just listened to the stories coming through on the phone and wondered if we were experiencing the last days of the old Wild West.

Arrest that Policeman!

I was the Alert Force Commander, on Alert for a week at a time in Galena. We wore our flight suits, including our pistols and security badges, as we could be scrambled at any moment. We had to be airborne within five minutes, but really we usually got airborne in about two and a half minutes. We were fast! Meanwhile we sat around, read books, played cards, or watched movies or phoned home once or twice during the week to check on how things were going with the wife and kids.

I was on the phone to Midge when I heard running footsteps. Three air policemen burst into the Alert Lounge with drawn pistols. "I got a problem—gotta go!" I said and hung up on Midge. "Show me your badges!" the air policeman demanded. I don't like looking into loaded pistols. We showed our badges, and the policeman seemed reasonably satisfied but highly agitated. The policemen did not have their own badges showing and were standing between the pilots and our planes, making it harder for us to scramble if the horn blew.

"Do you recognize me?" I asked the policeman. "Yes, Sir, you are the Alert Force Commander." "Then show me YOUR badges." "I don't have to show MY badge!" snapped the policeman. "Yes, you do, or I'll place you under arrest!" I snapped back. "I'll call the Sergeant of the Guard" said the policeman. "Do that, and tell him to call the Base Commander, too!" I ordered. The policeman grabbed his radio and said: "The pilots are arresting ME!" In a few minutes there were top sergeants and officers there to explain the situation. There was some sort of an Air Police exercise and they had told the police that there were intruders in the Alert Hangar — but they neglected to say that it was just an exercise! They came in expecting to find Russians. I said I didn't like looking into the barrels of loaded pistols. The Base Commander promised that it would never happen again.

Alaska Earthquake

Good Friday, March 27, 1964. I was at the base Photo Hobby Shop alone in the darkroom developing pictures. I heard a rumble, then the building shook and the darkroom safelight went out. The quake continued as I stumbled toward the door, hearing photo enlargers falling off their shelves all around me. The hot water pipes burst, spraying me with hot water as I found the door and stumbled out into the daylight. The parked cars in the parking lot were bouncing into each other; the steeple of the Base Chapel was whipping around so sharply that I felt sure that the steeple was about to fall.

An F-102 landing at Elmendorf AFB, Alaska. Note the drag chute, which we usually deployed in the air prior to touchdown. Deploying it in the air gave best effect, but made Flight Safety nervous!

The earthquake was rated at 8.5 on the Richter scale, the same as the great San Francisco earthquake. Electricity to the whole city failed in the first seconds of the quake, eliminating most sources of ignition so we had few fires. With electricity off, peoples' freezers began to thaw and there was no indoor cooking. Everyone got out their charcoal grills to grill their very best steaks before they spoiled. That evening our housing area looked like a big picnic as everyone charcoal grilled big steaks!

We didn't have heat, electricity, water, or telephones for several days. People sat in their cars listening to their radios report on rescue efforts. A sergeant and an airman were working at an Air Force warehouse. The airman was standing near the door while the sergeant was working at his desk in the middle of the warehouse. The earthquake hit suddenly and violently. The airman jumped out the door, and the roof of the warehouse came crashing down, trapping the sergeant inside. The airman got help. A big crane came and lifted pieces of the roof off the wreckage, looking for the sergeant. They found him, unhurt, in the footwell of his desk!

The Spirit of Attack

At the Elmendorf AFB Hospital, a man was getting some medical tests. The doctor gave him some shots, and put him in a dark room in a hospital bed with wheels. The nurse warned: "The shot will probably make you dizzy, but don't worry about it". The nurse turned out the light, closed the door and left the room. A few moments later, the great earthquake struck. The hospital shook violently, and cracks appeared in the walls. When the quake stopped, the nurse rushed back to the man she had just left. He exclaimed: "You said the shot would make me dizzy, but I could have sworn this bed was bouncing off the walls!"

The radio said that the air defense of the USA was not affected. That's only partly true. The bases at Eielson, Galena and King Salmon were not affected, but our home base at Elmendorf was hit. Aircraft in the alert hangars bounced into the walls, breaking their nose radomes. Big floodlights in the ceiling of our primary maintenance hangar broke loose and fell on the aircraft beneath. An F-102 looks rather awkward with a set of floodlights sticking out of its wing! We were back to normal in about a week.

The Alaska Earthquake struck on Good Friday, 1964. This school was on a level field; fortunately the children were on vacation. I took these photos myself of a school and a house near Elmendorf.

The Soviet TU-16 Badger frequently probed America's defenses. It had a retractable top turret and a tail gun. This tail turret has a gunner's position and a small radar dome which provided radar range to target. The tail guns are "caged" in the UP position, pointing at the sky. Caged guns indicate to our fighters that the Badger is not threatening us. The Badger below has Egyptian Air Force markings and carries two large white air-to-surface cruise missiles. Cruise missiles made it essential for us to intercept Soviet bombers as far as possible from our borders, before they could launch these missiles. Photos from Wikipedia.

Page 26 — **Bruce Gordon Stories**

Pilotless F-102

One day Capt. Bart Lynn and Lt. Colonel Joe Rogers, our Squadron Commander, were having coffee in the 317th FIS lounge in Alaska. They discussed a Korean War event in which a pilot lost consciousness and his wingman was able to turn his airplane toward home by flying in very close formation, without the wings touching. Most fighter pilots have felt the pressure when their wingman flies too close. The rising air going over the wingman's wing can lift the leader's wing without physical contact. I've felt it often, and looked over to see an overzealous wingman flying just too close. It feels like he's pushing my airplane. I'd call: "Stop pushing!" and he'd back off. Bart and Col. Joe discussed the details. They wondered if one F-102 could "push" another F-102 and control where he was headed. They decided to test the theory.

They took two F-102's, with Col. Joe in the lead aircraft. When they were at a safe altitude, Col. Joe trimmed up his plane, then took his hands off the controls and folded his arms. Bart moved into close formation on the right, and Col. Joe's plane flipped into a left spiral down. Col. Joe kept his arms folded, and Bart dove in and behind to the other side of Col. Joe's plane. Bart moved in until he flipped Col. Joe in the other direction. After a few tries, Bart apparently got pretty good at it and was able to fly Col. Joe around more or less at will. Col. Joe kept his arms folded the whole time!

I was a young pilot in the 317th at the time, and heard the story third-hand. I probably got the details wrong, but the story fascinated me. I wanted to hear more, but I didn't feel comfortable asking the Squadron Commander about it. Bart Lynn was soon reassigned to the 326th FIS at Richards-Gebaur AFB near Kansas City, Missouri. I forgot about the event for a couple of years.

I was transferred from Alaska to Selfridge AFB in Michigan and soon was flying the F-106 with the 94th FIS. The 94th was sent on TDY (Temporary Duty) to Alaska, and soon I was back on Alert in the same bases and hangars that I had flown from earlier. One day a copy of *Interceptor* magazine arrived, with a stunning photo: two F-102's in formation, and there was no pilot in the lead F-102! The article said that Capt. Bart Lynn had turned a pilotless F-102 away from Kansas City by flying in close formation with it!

According to *Interceptor* magazine, on 19 March 1965 an F-102 on a routine mission experienced hydraulic failure. Both primary and secondary hydraulic system pressures dropped to zero. The pilot tried to get back home to Richards-Gebaur (Kansas City), but the controls started to lock up. He was given a heading to turn the aircraft toward an uninhabited area, then he ejected. Interceptor magazine, May 1965, page 7, says:

"Before any further details were reported, the squadron was notified that the Deuce was still squawking emergency and was being tracked by radar. The route being flown by the disabled aircraft resembled a triangular pattern so the immediate reaction was that the ejection report had been a bit premature. A couple of minutes later, the unit was told that the aircraft had turned toward home and now just about everyone was convinced that someone was yelling wolf for no apparent reason. The excitement began to subside and most of the jocks had returned to the coffee bar complaining in unison about how the word can get so garbled without any translation. Not all the guys had their chance to voice their candid opinions on this problem when the squadron received a collect commercial call. You guessed it. The pilot who ejected was checking in from a local farmhouse. Since everyone knows that Mother Bell has yet to put a phone in a 102, the bits and pieces began to jell and the panic factor rose abruptly . . ."

Captain Bart Lynn had just taken off from R-G and was vectored to intercept the pilotless F-102, which was headed straight for Kansas City. Bart moved into close formation, and turned the F-102 away from Kansas City. The experience he had gained flying Col. Joe around Alaska came into play as he maneuvered the pilotless F-102 around and got it to an uninhabited area. He then flew it around until it ran out of fuel and crashed in a wooded area.

What a fortunate twist of fate! Bart had the experience of flying Col. Joe around Alaska, and then happened to be taking off from R-G just at the moment when he was needed to turn a pilotless plane away from Kansas City! The Almighty had protected the people of Kansas City — and also appreciate the wonderful airmanship of Bart Lynn and his Spirit of Attack!

The Spirit of Attack

The Lead F-102 Has No Pilot!
This is not a drone - the pilot had bailed out, plane heads for Kansas City
Capt. Bart Lynn turns plane away from KC using wing pressures
Interceptor Magazine, USAF Photo
This is the most amazing aviation photo that I've ever seen!

Selfridge AFB

In September 1964 I was transferred to Selfridge AFB by Mt. Clemons, Michigan, north of Detroit and joined the 94th Fighter Interceptor Squadron. This was the famous "Hat-in-the-Ring" squadron that Captain Eddie Rickenbacker had commanded during WW I, and saw heavy combat in P-38 fighters in Europe during WW II. The F-106 was very fast and had long range, so the 94th was sent on temporary duty to Alaska — and I was pulling Alert in the same alert hangars that I had been in with the F-102 a year earlier. The F-106 could reach out farther than the F-102. That long range brought risks—one night I was flying alone over the Arctic Ocean, more than a hundred miles north of Point Barrow, Alaska, waiting for a Russian bomber which didn't come. If I had bailed out for any reason, I would have died on the arctic icepack.

Night Flight

A good way to test the First Wing's F-106 aircraft and crews was to fly night exercises. The night was cold and snow covered the ground; a thick layer of clouds was moving into Michigan with light snowfall. My wife and children were asleep at home. As the poster said: "SLEEP TIGHT TONIGHT—YOUR AIR FORCE IS AWAKE".

AIRBORNE ORDER: 0130 HOURS, VECTOR 360, BUSTER ANGELS 40. The Airborne Order (instead of a Scramble) gave us a takeoff time so we didn't have to rush. Twenty minutes before takeoff time, I climbed into the cockpit and put on my frozen helmet. Everything was ready. I gave a hand signal to the crewchief, then started the jet engine. As the engine started, the voltage and hydraulic pressure gauges came up to normal. The aircraft became a living, breathing machine; a single-seat fighter, the best in the world. It was my body — I was its brain. I quickly did routine tests—I pushed a test switch which turned off the AC and DC power, simulating a failure and causing all but a few lights to go out and the instruments to seize. A moment later, the Emergency Power generator came on, and the instruments instantly returned to normal. I switched back to normal power and turned on the radar. All was ready; I signaled the crewchief to pull the chocks, and I taxied to the runway.

The radio cackled with instructions as I closed the canopy and turned up the cabin heat. My physical world was a very small cockpit with barely room to turn my head; the instruments glowed reassuringly. My mental world was expansive—the radar sweep showed me land and aircraft about twenty miles away. I knew that the weather was getting worse, and snow was moving in—but it was a routine winter snow, not expected to cause real problems. I would fly alone—there was no wingman, no copilot.

I taxied onto the runway and held the brakes as I pushed up the throttle. The whine of the jet engine became a roar; the aircraft strained against the brakes—one last check of the instruments and I released the brakes. A second later, I lit the afterburner—sudden energy pushed from behind, and the fighter rolled, then raced down the runway between the lights. About a hundred miles per hour and I raised the nose off the runway; seconds later I was airborne. The lights of the airport disappeared behind and suddenly all lights vanished as I entered the low clouds. The instruments told me everything I needed to know—the artificial horizon showed that I was climbing and turning to my assigned heading vector of 360 degrees—due north. In a couple of minutes I broke out on top of the clouds—there was a bright moon—the world looked very peaceful.

The radio barked commands and the computer presented key information. There was an American bomber coming in from Canada as part of our exercise. It was pretending to be a Russian bomber; my job was to intercept it and simulate shooting it down.

There! The radar picked up a blip—then another, then another! The sky was full of targets—but were they real? No, they were bursts of chaff. Where was the real target? Oh, there it was—it was a bit smaller than the false targets, but was moving — the puffs of chaff hung motionless in the air. I locked onto the real target. He turned and dumped more chaff in an effort to escape, but could not get away. I pushed up the throttle and closed at the speed of sound; the computer calculated the closure rates; I squeezed the trigger and at the right instant the computer generated the fire signal. The missile bays (which look like bomb bays) opened in a split second—the missile rails extended and the training missiles looked at the target, recording a "hit" on their data tapes—the rails retracted and the doors closed with a thud. I broke off the attack and turned for home—mission accomplished!

The Spirit of Attack

The F-106 looked like the F-102, but was much more powerful. The engine intakes were set back farther and the tail was squared off, not pointed like the F-102. It was highly maneuverable and could go twice the speed of sound in level flight. It carried four guided missiles (2 radar and two IR) plus an unguided rocket with a nuclear warhead. Its radar could change frequencies rapidly and randomly, making it almost impossible to jam. The F-102 and F-106 both had infrared tracking systems. I took this photo near Naha, Okinawa, Japan in 1969.

I tuned my radio to Approach Control and they gave me instructions to get back home. I flew back south and descended toward the wide, flat tops of the clouds which were illuminated by the bright moonlight. The weather at home was poor: 300 foot overcast, one mile visibility in snow. Not too bad—I had confidence in my ability to make the instrument approach. I descended into the clouds, and was once again in total darkness except for the warm glow of my instruments. As I got lower, I switched my radio to Final Approach; I was now fifteen hundred feet above the ground; I put down my landing gear and turned on my landing lights. The lights showed nothing but snow streaming toward me from the darkness ahead. No sweat—just follow the instruments, and listen to the radio. "You're intercepting the glide path now, start your descent". I was on final approach; I pulled back the throttle and started down.

BAM! WHAM! The fighter shuddered with sudden power surges—then the AC and DC electrical power failed! My radar set and computer died instantly. Only the battery was left, giving a few critical red lights, powering the radio, and lighting up a maze of warning lights. The vital instruments jumped violently and stopped, with big "OFF" flags; the artificial horizon turned upside down and went "OFF". My heart was in my throat—what had happened? *Which way was up?*

My mind raced with the thoughts of a fighter pilot who sees death: what can I do? A man without instruments does the wrong things and quickly enters a "graveyard spiral". The radio snapped out the warning: "You're going 50, 100, 200 feet below the glidepath. PULL UP! PULL UP!" I took my hands off the controls—I didn't know which way was up, so I'd let God fly the plane. My hands quivered over the ejection handles—it was time to eject!

My mind raced wildly—**Emergency Power**! It should have come on automatically—and I had tested it before takeoff—why wasn't it on? In desperation I reached over and pushed the Emergency Power Test switch. It worked! The lights came on suddenly, the "OFF" flags disappeared, and the instruments snapped to life!

The artificial horizon showed me in a nose-down dive to the right. I rolled to the left and pulled back on the stick—just as I dropped through the bottom of the clouds, only 300 feet above the ground! I pulled hard, barely missing the ground, and there was a house in front of me! I just got over the roof of the house, and I could look inside a second-floor window, where a light was on, and I could see a man sitting at a desk! A moment later, I was back in the dark clouds, following the radio instructions as if nothing had happened. In a couple of minutes I again broke out below the clouds, but this time there was the friendly runway ahead of me.

I landed and taxied in; the crewchief showed me where to park. I opened the canopy and shut down the engine, and sat there in the cockpit, trying to collect my thoughts. "Flight OK, Sir?" the crewchief asked. I slowly took off my helmet; my clothes were soaked with sweat; the cold breeze and snow felt somehow refreshing—I was still alive!

The Spirit of Attack

Major Robert L. Smith, my Flight Commander, flying an F-106 by Mt. McKinley, Alaska in 1967. I flew the F-106 in the same Alaskan skies that I had previously flown the F-102. The F-106 had more range and we could intercept Russians 100 miles north of Point Barrow, over the Arctic Ocean.

Bomarc Kill

21 March, 1967; Tyndall AFB, Florida. I preflighted my F-106A carefully, with special attention to the one AIM-4G missile loaded in the missile bay. The infrared missile would be put to its most challenging test: shoot down a Bomarc missile on a head-on attack. The Bomarc would be at 55,000 feet altitude traveling at Mach 2.3, and I would be at 45,000 feet at Mach 1.5 going directly at it. The closing speed of Mach 3.8 was near the design limit for the F-106 fire control system; this live test would prove that the F-106 could meet its design goals. So far, nobody had been able to hit a Bomarc, which was a "pilotless interceptor" missile controlled by the ground and designed to hit high-flying enemy bombers. Today I would try to shoot it down.

"DOORS CLEAR!" With a warning shout and a careful look around, I pushed a switch in the wheel well. WHAM! The pneumatically-operated missile-bay doors slammed shut in a fraction of a second. The missile was now secure in air-conditioned comfort in the missile bay; it would not be exposed to the brutal forces of nature again until an instant before firing. It was an infrared missile, known to be very accurate — but what could an infrared missile see on a head-on attack? The engineers told us that the Bomarc would be going so fast that its skin would heat and make a good target. The Bomarc had better be a good target — the missile did not have a proximity fuse, and had to make a direct hit to detonate the warhead.

The crewchief, A1C Thompson, helped me strap in and wished me luck. A blast of compressed air, followed by the whine of a J-75 engine starting, showed that my leader had started. Colonel Hugh J. Martin, Squadron Commander of the 94th FIS, was leading our two-ship mission. He would get first crack at the Bomarc. Colonel Martin had an AIM-4F missile, which was radar-directed and was expected to have the best chance of hitting the Bomarc on the head-on attack. He outranked me, so I would fly in trail behind him.

I pressed the starter button and watched the engine gauges come to life; I switched the radar on and carefully checked it out. The single-engine, one-man F-106 seemed alive; a fantastic fighting machine built around an excellent radar set. In a couple of minutes we were taxiing, passing two F-104s near the end of the runway. The F-104s would actually get the first shots at the Bomarc. Their Sidewinder missiles had to be fired up the tailpipe of the target. The F-104s would take off and accelerate to Mach 2 going in the same direction as the Bomarc; the ground controller would fly the Bomarc right over their heads at Mach 2.3 and the F-104's would hose off Sidewinders as it passed.

Close canopy — taxi onto the runway — hold brakes & run up engine to full military power. The plane vibrated with power like a tiger straining at a leash. I looked over at Colonel Martin and nodded that I was ready — he released his brakes and lit his afterburner — the roar of power filled my senses. Twenty seconds later, I roared down the runway behind him. The Gulf of Mexico was beautiful as we climbed to altitude; I turned away from Colonel Martin and switched to a different ground radar controller. Soon we were orbiting separately at 41,000 feet, waiting for the show to begin.

Bruce Gordon Stories

The Spirit of Attack

My aircraft crewchief and my radar crewchief hoist me onto their shoulders after I shot down a Bomarc missile with a missile.

The Bomarc was a long-range ramjet-powered guided missile which could carry a nuclear warhead. It was launched vertically by powerful booster rockets, which accelerated it to the speed needed to start its two ramjet engines. It climbed to about 65,000 feet and came down on its target at about Mach 2.5. We used it as a high-speed target because it was near the design limitations of the F-106 fire control system. I took this photo of a Bomarc at the AF Museum.

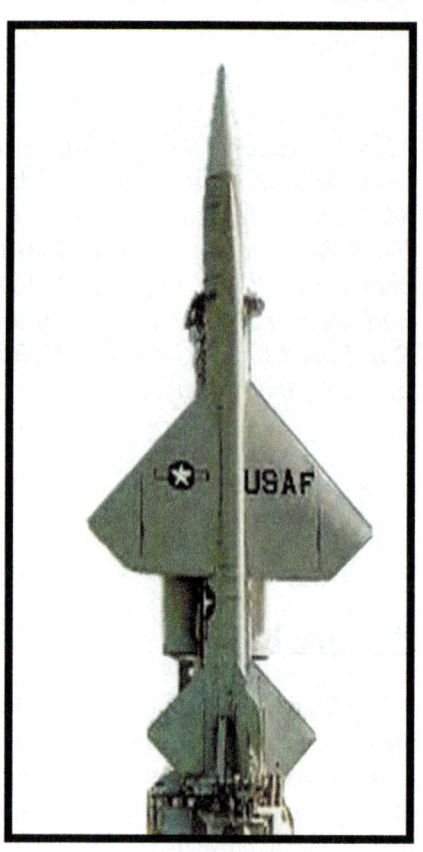

"BOMARC AIRBORNE!" It was over two hundred miles away as I turned to meet the target. My radar picked up Colonel Martin about twenty miles ahead of me. I lit my afterburner and began to accelerate; Mach 1.0; Mach 1.1; Mach 1.2; Mach 1.3. The F-106 continued to accelerate, the airframe vibrating with supersonic speed. The radio came alive as the F-104s started their attack; one fired a Sidewinder but the Bomarc ran away from it. The target was 100 miles away; I could already see its contrail as it reached 50,000 feet and turned toward me. I reached Mach 1.5 and swiftly climbed to 45,000 feet—a safe altitude below the oncoming Bomarc.

I could see the Bomarc's contrail distinctly at fifty miles, coming directly at me. Colonel Martin's contrail passed just under it, but he couldn't get his radar locked on and couldn't fire. When Colonel Martin was safely past the target, my controller called: "CLEAR TO FIRE!"

The Bomarc was on my radar, closing very rapidly. I'd never seen a target move so fast. I broke the safety wire and armed my missile, quickly trying to lock onto the target while instinctively continuing my climb into the Bomarc's path. The radar locked on, the target marker circle collapsed and I squeezed the trigger. WHAM! The plane shuddered as the missile bay doors opened and the missile extended into the supersonic airstream. WOOSH! I heard the missile ignite right under me and saw it race toward the Bomarc.

Time seemed to go into slow motion as the missile guided right at the onrushing Bomarc. I watched in amazement, like a spectator in a theater — while continuing to climb to get a better look. Split seconds later the missile met the Bomarc — there was a huge explosion and a ball of fire as I saw it hit the Bomarc's left engine intake and detonate. The Bomarc's left wing blew off and it snapped inverted and dived onto me. My mouth opened in fright as the Bomarc passed just over my canopy, a ball of fire that seemed to fill my whole world.

In an instant, it was gone. "SPLASH ONE BOMARC!" My victory call was mingled with horror as I noted that I had climbed above 48,000 feet and had nearly been killed by my target which dove when it was hit. Out of afterburner, slow down and descend; I was breathing hard with excessive adrenaline as I sought to regain composure. When I got down on the ground, I'd have to act like a cool fighter pilot — but my mind's eye still carries an instant picture of a fireball passing just over my head at hypersonic speed.

MACE Kill

In 1968, several generals were looking at PK (Probability of Kill) tables for the F-106 and its missiles. What was the probability that an F-106 would get off the ground and not abort for maintenance? What was the probability that it would find the target and actually fire missiles? What was the probability that the missiles would guide and hit the target? Those probability tables were the basis for our tactics of committing two F-106's against each attacking Russian bomber. The older F-86D committed four per bomber. The generals saw the high PK for the F-106 and were thinking of using only one F-106 per attacking bomber. If the tables were wrong, the air defense of America would be in jeopardy.

The tables showed a high PK, but one general argued that the tables were based entirely on test conditions, and that the aircraft and missiles were carefully prepared for the tests. Most of the tests involved single missiles, and the targets had extra radar reflectors to make them look like bombers, or had extra heat sources to make them better infrared targets. What was the probability that routine F-106s with standard missiles could shoot down a realistic target? They finally decided on a special test. They would take two actual F-106s on Alert and see how they performed in a simulated wartime scenario.

A T-33 landed, unannounced, at Selfridge AFB with two Colonels aboard. They went directly to our Alert Hangar and impounded two of the four F-106s that we had on Alert. The planes were fully loaded, with two radar missiles, two infrared missiles, and one nuclear weapon. Under the watchful eyes of the Colonels, the radar missiles and the nuclear weapon were removed, leaving only the two infrared missiles. Because of crew rest restrictions, the Squadron Commander was told to replace the Alert pilots with two men who were fully rested.

The Squadron Commander could send anyone he wanted. He picked me because I had proven skill by shooting down the BOMARC a few months earlier, and he picked Captain Arnie Voit because he was the best radar man we had. Arnie and I were called up and sent out to the Alert Hangar for our briefing.

The Colonels told us the rules of the test: We would fly south to Tyndall AFB, Florida, where we would land, refuel, and be briefed on range safety procedures. There would be two targets: a MACE cruise missile, and a backup BQM-34 drone, without any extra reflectors or heat generators, in case the MACE did not launch properly. The key to the test was: THERE WOULD BE ABSOLUTELY NO MAINTENANCE ON THE AIRCRAFT OR THE MISSILES, other than refueling and normal servicing, before firing the missiles. On the other hand, we would treat this as a wartime situation and would fly as we would in wartime. It was a fighter pilot's dream—we could use any tactics that we wished. I was the senior ranking officer, so I would lead the flight.

Arnie and I went to the planes and started up. As soon as I turned on the radar, I noted that the "range gate" was drifting badly. That is how the pilot tells the radar which target to track — without a functioning range gate, I could not lock the radar onto the target. That was a simple screwdriver adjustment for a radar man, but maintenance was prohibited. We could use any tactics we wanted, so I decided that I could use the F-106's infrared tracking system for angle while getting firing range from the radar. We took off for Florida without any maintenance and I said nothing about my radar problem.

When we got to Florida, Arnie said that his radar was working fine and that he really, REALLY wanted to get the first shot at the MACE! He pointed out that I had got to shoot down the BOMARC, and he wanted a piece of that MACE! I agreed to give him the first shot, and we went in for our safety briefing. The MACE and the backup BQM-34 drone would be launched out over the Gulf of Mexico; a photographer would ride in the back seat of an F-101 to record the test.

Captain Arnie Voit and F-106

The Spirit of Attack

Our planes had been refueled, so we started engines. My radar range gate was still unacceptable, but I did not try to get it fixed. My radar search was working fine, but I could not track with radar. It was a beautiful day as we flew out over the Gulf of Mexico and were directed toward our targets; Arnie took the lead and went after the MACE while I flew a loose "fighting wing" position where I could attack immediately if Arnie missed.

We picked up the MACE on radar and swung into a stern attack. Arnie attacked aggressively and fired his two infrared missiles. The missiles were supposed to "ripple fire" a quarter of a second apart, but they both launched at the same instant. The missiles were about four feet apart in the missile bay, and they stayed right beside each other as they raced toward the MACE, homing in on its tailpipe. As they reached the MACE, the two missiles tried to crowd into the tailpipe at the same time and hit each other.

MACE cruise missile at the Air Force Museum. It was launched by a booster rocket, was powered by a turbojet engine, and could carry a nuclear weapon.

The two missiles exploded a few feet behind the MACE! The blast flipped the MACE tail-up, and for a second it dove toward the Gulf waters. Then, the MACE's autopilot took over and it returned to level flight, only a few feet above the water! The MACE was still flying, so I swung in to attack. As I attacked, I noticed that the MACE was slowing down, and I realized that the blast had "flamed out" the MACE's engine. With no pilot it could not re-start its engine. I held off my attack and watched as the MACE's autopilot tried very hard to keep that cruise missile in the air. It went slower and dropped ever closer to the water. Finally it crashed into the blue Gulf waters in a great splash of white spray. Arnie Voit had shot down a cruise missile under realistic combat conditions.

The BQM-34 drone had been launched as a backup target, and I was directed to shoot it down. I used my sweep radar to find the target, and locked on my infrared tracking system as I closed behind the target. Range to the target was difficult to read precisely on my scope; the target looked smaller than I thought it should, so I closed a bit inside the ideal firing range before pulling the trigger.

My two infrared missiles ripple-fired a quarter of a second apart and both guided on the drone's tailpipe. The second missile was behind the first missile, got in its smoke trail, and lost track of the target. It corkscrewed away down into the Gulf. The first missile hit the drone directly in the tailpipe and exploded in a big fireball. Pieces of the drone went in all directions, and I suddenly realized that I was a lot closer to it than I wanted to be! I pulled up hard but flew through the edge of the fireball. I did not feel any impacts from pieces of the drone, although bits of paint were scraped from my aircraft.

BQM-34 Target Drone. It was launched by a booster rocket and had a turbojet engine. It was too expensive to use only once. The Army used it to tow banner targets for anti-aircraft gunners. The Air Force usually fired missiles with inert warheads and put flares on the wingtips to keep the missiles from hitting the drone. When hit, its engine would shut off and a parachute would deploy to bring it down. Air Force photo.

We had scrambled two F-106's in a wartime scenario, and we had shot down two realistic targets. The F-106 had proved itself; tactics were changed so that in the future we would commit only one F-106 at a time against each Russian bomber. Shortly thereafter, Arnie Voit came down with a fatal case of Multiple Sclerosis. I was having breakfast with him in the Squadron one morning when he said that he couldn't feel his leg. He went to the doctor, and was soon in the hospital. He medically retired from the Air Force. Arnie his wife Margie left Selfridge AFB in May 1969, just before the rest of us went to Korea. Even fighter pilots in the best of health can be struck down in their prime. I remember Arnie as an aggressive, skilled pilot who had the spirit of attack and was the one who shot down the MACE!

Flight Test

My interest in aircraft systems led to my being assigned as a Flight Test pilot in Quality Control for both the T-33 and the F-106. This is not "Test Flying" in the commonly perceived sense of testing new aircraft, but testing existing aircraft after they had major maintenance, such as engine change. These were called "Functional Check Flights". Selfridge AFB had a contractor performing major T-33 maintenance, and I flew many T-33 flight tests. The most interesting problem was once when I had fuel feeding problems, which maintenance could not explain. I flew the T-33 on three flights and got weird fuel problems. Finally they opened the fuselage fuel tank (just behind the cockpit) and found a set of wooden chocks in the fuel tank! Yes, that's right—wooden chocks, the things that you use to keep the wheels from rolling when the aircraft is parked. Apparently someone was doing maintenance in the empty fuel tank (which is surprisingly large) and brought in a pair of chocks to sit on while doing maintenance on the many floats which control the flow of fuel from the wing tanks. When he finished adjusting the floats, he sealed the fuel tank with the chocks inside! The big wooden chocks floated in the fuel, bumping into the floats and causing various problems. That's a good example of why they have an experienced pilot fly the aircraft after major maintenance.

As Quality Control Officer for the F106, I was involved as we were X-raying aircraft structures for possible cracks. When we looked at the X-rays of one F-106, we could clearly see some tools. We examined the photo closely, and went to the aircraft trying to find the tools. After a lot of work, we decided that the tools were riveting tools left in the aircraft when it was originally constructed. The tools were sealed inside the aircraft structure and could not be removed without tearing out most of the aircraft's hydraulic and pneumatic systems. We held a maintenance meeting to determine what should be done. My advice was that the tools had been there for years in an empty spot of the fuselage, and they couldn't do any damage. The Chief of Maintenance agreed, and we just put a note in the permanent aircraft records about the tools. We were concerned that, if the aircraft ever crashed and an aircraft accident board examined the wreckage, they're sure have some questions about where those tools came from!

During one F-106 test flight, my radio failed. They replaced the radio, and it failed again. After the third replacement, we tore open the whole area near the radio and found a very nice metal flashlight lying among the wires. The batteries on the flashlight were still good, so it had not been there long. I passed the word to Maintenance that anyone who wanted their flashlight back should come and ask me for it. Nobody claimed the flashlight, so I kept and used it for years.

About ten years later (1975) I was a Quality Control officer at Wright-Patterson AFB where we did major work on many kinds of aircraft. One day I got an emergency call: after a reported fuel feeding problem in a C-130 cargo plane, we had drained the fuel and opened one of their very large wing fuel tanks. A maintenance man had gone into the tank and reported that he had found a dead body in the tank! I rushed down and we got the Air Police, then went back into the fuel tank to remove the body. It turned out not to be a body, but was a heavy Air Force coat with nobody in it. The coat must have been left in the tank during major maintenance several years earlier.

Back to Selfridge AFB in 1964. Our F-106 tires were a big problem and had to be replaced often. We were finally issued a new brand of tires that were supposed to be much better. Two days after we got the new tires, I was called out to look at the new tires on an F-106 that had landed that afternoon. The tire treads were in shreds, and my Quality Control people were busy writing up an emergency message to withdraw all the new tires from use. I could hardly believe that new tires had failed so quickly, and I looked in the aircraft forms. I saw that the pilot who last flew the plane was a good friend of mine. I went back to my office and called him on the phone. "Was there anything unusual about your landing this afternoon?" I asked. "Why do you ask?" was his cautious reply. I told him about the tires. "I'll tell you if you promise not to tell anyone", he said. I promised. "I landed short", he confessed. I thanked him and drove out to the approach end of the runway. There, in the overrun, I saw the impact marks of F-106 tires that broke several inches deep into the asphalt overrun and led directly to the lip of the concrete runway! I was surprised that the tires had not blown out on impact. I drove back to my office, where my Quality Control men had an emergency message on my desk for my signature, telling all F-106 units to withdraw the new tires from use. I thanked my men for their quick work, then tore up the message and threw it in the trash. I explained that there were "special circumstances" about the tire failure, which I was not going to discuss. We had no more trouble with the new tires.

A test flight after an engine change required a high-speed run to Mach 2.0, twice the speed of sound. Air intakes are very important during supersonic flight, as the engine turbine blades cannot handle supersonic air. All supersonic aircraft need some method of keeping supersonic air from hitting the engine compressor blades. A characteristic of a shock wave is that the air is supersonic on one side of the shock wave, and subsonic on the other side. The F-106 had "variable ramps" which were driven by hydraulics and moved to change the geometry of the air intakes as you went faster. The moving variable ramps kept the shock wave ahead of the engine compressor blades, so the engine always swallowed subsonic air. One day I was accelerating past Mach 1.95 when I heard a strange sound, like the engine bearings were failing. A moment later, WHAM! The plane shook with an explosion and seemed to fly sideways, barely under control. I couldn't bail out at supersonic speed because the wind would rip my body to pieces, so I came out of afterburner and cautiously slowed down. The plane was flying OK, so I returned to Selfridge and landed. I looked deeply into maintenance manuals, and found a simple statement: If the variable ramps do not function correctly, the shock wave can hit the engine compressor blades. The engine can't swallow supersonic air, so it "compressor stalls". It coughs and spits the shock wave out of one intake while the air still comes in the intake on the other side of the aircraft, making the aircraft seem to fly sideways. The warning that this is about to happen is a noise "like a swarm of bees", followed by a violent compressor stall, but no aircraft damage occurs. The manual continued: "This is called Stall Buzz, which is a misnomer. It is much more than a buzz, and is frightening to anyone who experiences it". I'll second that!

Supersonic Target

The F-101 base at Columbus, Ohio was having a big ORI (Operational Readiness Inspection), and I was assigned to fly as supersonic target for their exercise. I took off from Selfridge (Detroit) and climbed while flying southwest to South Bend, Indiana. At that point I had reached 45,000 feet altitude and turned east toward Columbus, Ohio. I lit my afterburner and went supersonic. I was very interested in the performance of my variable ramps, and noted details such as the brief surge in hydraulic pressure at Mach 1.2 as the computer activated the variable ramps. At Mach 1.4 the variable ramps were visibly moving, and I could see them by looking hard over my shoulder into the engine intakes. Very interesting, but my job was to be target. I looked below me and saw two F-101's coming in for an intercept; they were at about 35,000 feet and their contrails showed they were in full afterburner. The F-101's top speed was published as Mach 1.85, so I slowed back down to Mach 1.2 to give them a chance to catch me. I watched them fall behind and two more F-101's joined the attack, so I slowed down to Mach 1.1 with all four F-101's behind me. By now I had reached the end of my target run so I came out of afterburner and started down to land at the F-101's home base. Their control tower said that there were four F-101's coming in with emergency fuel and asked if I could let the F-101's land first. I said OK, as I had plenty of fuel and weather was good. I circled while the F-101's landed, then I came in and landed.

When I taxied in to park, an Air Force staff car came to my plane. As I climbed out of the plane, some officers were waiting for me. "How's the war going?" I asked cheerfully. "The F-106's are winning", they replied bitterly. They explained that the top speed of the F-101 was Mach 1.4 with external fuel tanks and could barely make Mach 1.2 when turning. They had been told that the F-106 target would be barely supersonic, about Mach 1.05, so they chose a stern attack instead of a frontal attack in order to have an easier "kill". As they dropped behind me, they could close with me, but they were at 35,000 feet and I was at 45,000 feet. They would get just about to firing range and start to pull up to "fire" their missiles, but as they pulled up they slowed down and would fall back out of range. All four F-101's stayed in full afterburner and chased me across Ohio until they ran low on fuel and had to break off the attack, calling an "MI" or Missed Intercept. According to ORI rules, very few MI's were permitted, and must be charged either to the pilots, to the radar, or to the ground intercept radar. The failure was caused by their decision to make a stern attack, rather than a frontal attack. They had chosen a "safe" tactic instead of showing the "Spirit of Attack". Four missed intercepts were not permitted, and they would fail their ORI. By the time I got back to Selfridge there was an angry message from their Commander to my Commander, saying that I had caused them to fail the ORI. When called to explain my actions, I told the truth. My Operations Officer said that I had been briefed to fly at only Mach 1.05, but he had never specified any speed — only to fly slow enough so the F-101's could catch me. I thought that Mach 1.1 was a reasonable target speed. My lack of knowledge of their limitations had caused a squadron to fail its ORI, and had caused bad feelings with the F-101 squadron. Bad scene.

I become a UFO

I was assigned to fly a T-33 as low-level target for one of our late-night exercises. My aircraft was loaded with two chaff dispensers full of those little zinc needles (in the early days it was strips of aluminium foil) packed in packages which look like an aircraft on radar. I took off from Selfridge after midnight and flew my assigned target route. I frequently switched radio frequencies trying to find if any fighters were coming after me, but the night was silent. I had turned back and was just south of Toledo when I heard an F-101's radio report indicating that he was going after a low-level target. That would be me! There was open farmland ahead of me, so I descended to the lowest safe altitude for night and began to drop chaff. I kept my bright flashing lights on for reasons of safety. The F-101 was still coming after me. A very high rate of dropping chaff can often break the radar lock of a fighter, so I turned both my chaff tanks to maximum and really poured out the chaff. The F-101 was able to stay locked on in spite of the flood of chaff. He called "MA" (Mission Accomplished). To thumb his nose at me, he came roaring just over my cockpit then lit both his afterburners, pulled up and did a victory roll. His afterburners and flashing anticollision lights made a nice spectacle in the night sky. I continued back to Selfridge and landed without incident.

A day later the Detroit Daily News reported that a UFO had been spotted just south of Toledo. A farmer had heard his dogs barking at a skunk or raccoon, and had gone out to investigate. Suddenly he heard a loud roar and looked up to see flashing lights and two balls of fire going straight up! When dawn came, he saw that his field was covered with small metallic needles . . .

Captain Eddie Rickenbacker in WW I

Eddie Rickenbacker was America's "Ace of Aces" in WW I and his favorite aircraft was the Spad bi-wing fighter. He was a true hero and was one of the founders of the Indianapolis Speedway just before WW I. When he wanted to learn to fly, his mother told him: "All right, but promise that you'll always fly slow and stay close to the ground". After the war, he founded an airline. Many books were written about him.

"Captain Eddie" was Commander of the 94th Fighter Squadron. He chose the "Hat-in-the-Ring" emblem for the 94th fighters. We in the 94th were thrilled when Captain Eddie accepted our invitation and came to Selfridge AFB in 1967 for the 50th anniversary of Selfridge AFB, to see a rebuilt flyable Spad and to attend a formal "Dining In" dinner. Captain Eddie received full VIP treatment. He prided himself in keeping up with technology and most of his public comments were in support of hi-tech activities and space flight.

We 94th Squadron pilots, though, wanted to hear about his WW I exploits. We convened a special breakfast in our Squadron dining room, just for Eddie and Squadron fighter pilots (although a few Colonels managed to crash the party). When Eddie spoke, it was about space travel again. Finally I could stand it no longer and asked him to tell us a war story from WW I.

Eddie asked: "How long would it take for you to take off, shoot down an enemy airplane, and land — under ideal conditions?" I said it would take five minutes to scramble, at least ten minutes to locate and shoot down the enemy plane, and another ten minutes to get back and land. At least twenty-five minutes.

"Five minutes" he said firmly. We muttered in disbelief, so he told this story: The Squadron was in France and was given French Nieuport bi-wing fighters to fly, but they didn't have any guns. The Squadron set up on a field and began training flights, but could not fight without guns. The Germans knew they were there, and every morning an observation plane would fly down the runway taking pictures, make a right turn and fly back to the German lines.

One afternoon a truck arrived with guns for their Nieuports. They worked all afternoon and through the night installing the guns on their planes. Captain Eddie had just finished installing and test-firing his guns and was still sitting in the cockpit with the engine ticking over when the air raid siren blew. The German observation plane was coming! Captain Eddie opened his throttle and took off as the observation plane flew over his head. As it started its right turn, Captain Eddie cut it off, pulled up and shot it down! He continued his turn around to the right and landed. He taxied in, and logged just five minutes of flying time!

The Spirit of Attack

Captain Eddie Rickenbacker with his Spad in 1918.

He was America's "Ace of Aces" with 26 kills, and was the first commander of the 94th Fighter Squadron with its "Hat in the Ring" emblem.

Captain Eddie Rickenbacker at Selfridge AFB, Michigan in 1967 with a Spad fighter. The Spad had been re-built and was flown for the occasion. I wondered what we'd have done if Eddie said he wanted to fly it! The Spad was faster than I expected, flying so fast that an Army helicopter (assigned as a safety chase) was unable to keep up with it.

When the Air Force Museum heard that we were actually flying the airplane, they took it from us for the Museum, where it is today. They removed our "Hat in the Ring" emblem and replaced it with the Indian Head, the original emblem of the 94th. We pilots wanted the "Hat in the Ring", but the Museum never asked for our opinion.

Me with a replica French Nieuport at a 94th Squadron reunion in 1997. This is the type of fighter that Captain Eddie was flying when he shot down a German plane in WW I and logged only five minutes of flying time!

The Hat-in-Ring 94th Squadron patch, used by Eddie Rickenbacker, is used by the 94th Tactical Fighter Squadron, with F-22 stealth fighters, today."

Historical note: The Spad was British and the Nieuport was French. No American-designed & built aircraft fought in WW I, although we produced large numbers of American engines which were used in British and French aircraft.

The Spirit of Attack

Aerial Combat Tactics

The war in Vietnam was heating up, and Soviet MiG-17 and MiG-21 fighters were giving our F-4's a hard time. Air Force aerial combat training had always been with fighters of the same type because it was safer to have pilots with the same training work together to demonstrate specific maneuvers. A dogfight between fighters of the same type was a test of pilots, but nobody had a performance advantage and equally skilled pilots would end up chasing each other in a tight circle which kept descending as the tight turns reduced their airspeed, right down to the ground. The MiG-17 could out-turn almost anybody, but could not fly faster than sound. The MiG-19 could fly Mach 1.2 and could out-turn the F-4 but couldn't match the F-4's Mach 2 speed. The MiG-21 went Mach 2 and could out-turn the F-4, but it had poor radar. Tactics would have to change depending on your enemy.

The US Navy was doing quite well with its "Top Gun" program, flying different types of fighters against each other. The Navy's combat success was credited to its training between unlike aircraft, but improvements could be made. At this time, the Air Force Academy came up with the concept of "energy maneuverability" which related engine power to aircraft weight/wing area (wing loading). For example, our F-105 strike fighter had a very powerful engine (the same as the F-106's engine) but was very heavy and had a high wing loading, so it could go very fast at low altitudes but it could not turn very well. The MiG-17 had less power but had light wing loading, so it could turn but couldn't go so fast. The MiG-21 was the primary threat, both fast and with a light wing loading. The Air Force Academy created formulas and used computers to calculate which aircraft would be best at high or low altitudes, high or low speeds. The MiG-21 was the greatest threat to our F-4 air superiority fighters, so the Academy looked at the computer to tell them which Air Force aircraft was closest to the MiG-21 in energy maneuverability. Their computer analysis was clear: the F-106 was closest to the MiG-21.

Nobody had thought of the F-106 as an air superiority fighter. All of our training was in radar attacks against bombers; we had no training in fighter maneuvers. The F-4's had a fighter weapons school at Nellis AFB, Nevada and they were the experts in fighter tactics. The Air Force agreed to let the F-4 experts at Nellis try their skills against the F-106 and its untrained pilots. The F-4 jocks were in for a surprise!

The Air Force ordered four F-106 aircraft and six pilots from Selfridge AFB to Nellis for a special program. Once there, they showed us two movies about aerial combat tactics—that was our total training. Then we went to fly against the F-4 experts; they put F-106 pilots in the back seat of some F-4's so we could learn tactics as we flew. For the first week, their experience was

The MiG-17 was transonic with an afterburner and was very dangerous in a turning fight. It shot down some of our fighters during the Vietnam War. Never turn with a MiG-17! Photo from Flickr.

The MiG-21 flew Mach 2 and was best at medium-altitude turning fights. Fighter names start with "F", so the NATO code name was "Fishbed". AF Museum photo

America's primary fighter was the F-4. It was good at everything, but not best at anything. It could carry a heavy load of bombs or hold its own in a dogfight. It was fast when not carrying bombs or external tanks. USAF Photo

Bruce Gordon Stories

decisive, but after that the F-106 proved superior to the F-4 and we won the engagements. We learned to make the F-106 do things never considered before, such as the "rudder reversal". In full afterburner and pulling as many G's as we could, we would feed in top rudder and the F-106 would rotate so that our big delta wing would be against the wind, causing our airspeed to drop suddenly. The F-4 chasing us couldn't stop that fast, and would go whistling past us as we continued the rudder roll and dropped down on his tail! The F-4 experts couldn't believe the maneuver, and said it was impossible. We had learned that the F-106 was superior to the F-4, and began to train for fighter vs. fighter combat.

We started a program on Aerial Combat Training for all our F-106 pilots, and I became an instructor. We didn't know if the aircraft could stand the high G-forces that we were using. The F-4 pilots said that F-106 pilots couldn't take G's because we didn't have G-suits, which inflate to push the blood back into the head so a pilot doesn't black out. It turned out that the F-106's seat is mounted at an angle, so that high G's went across our body instead of from head to foot. These transverse G's can be tolerated well without a G-suit. The F-106's wings would bend under the G-forces and many of our wingtip lights would pop out of the wings, but they could be replaced easily. To everyone's surprise, our radar and advanced computers were not damaged by the G-forces.

Tumbling the F-106

We talked about what to do if an enemy is on your tail and you can't shake him; what is your "last ditch maneuver"? I had heard vague rumors that the F-106 could be "tumbled", end over end, like slow aerobatic planes do in a flying circus. I decided to try it as an experiment. It was stupid and I nearly lost the airplane, but this is how it went: I told my wingman to drop into firing position behind me as I lit the afterburner and went into a very hard turn to the left. We knew that the F-106 rudder would provide a reverse effect when under negative G's and the ailerons would provide an "adverse yaw" affect when under heavy G's. When my wingman said he was tracking me and was ready to fire, I suddenly crammed the stick into the left front corner and stomped on the right rudder pedal. The reaction was VIOLENT! The plane snapped so hard that my helmet hit the canopy rail and the world spun around me. I tried to count the number of times the sky and ground swapped positions, but it was all a blur. After what I guessed was three tumbles, I quickly returned the stick to its normal hard-turn position.

"ARE YOU OK?" My wingman called. My head was ringing from when my helmet hit the canopy, but the plane seemed to be flying all right. We landed and looked the plane over; there was no apparent damage. I asked what the maneuver looked like and whether it would have been an effective "last ditch maneuver". He said it was amazing to see, but my plane just rolled over and over right in front of him and never made him lose a firing position. He said that an enemy pilot might stop shooting just out of amazement at what he saw, but tumbling was not an effective last ditch maneuver. It was clearly very dangerous, so I never did it again.

F-106 vs. F-104

We were deployed to Tyndall AFB in Florida to try tactics against F-104's. For several weeks we flew missions simulating Vietnam combat. Four F-101's would simulate a "strike force" attacking North Vietnam; they would travel at maximum speed at low level. Eight F-106's would fly top cover for the "strike force". Four F-104's would simulate MiG-21's and attack us at high speed. To simulate a North Vietnamese strike, the F-104's would be told by radar about where we were, but we were not told anything about their position. The F-101, F-104, and F-106 pilots would gather in the morning and brief the total mission. We would then split up and make our own secret plans for tactics. The F-106's would take off first, because we had longer range and endurance than the others. The F-101's would move to a position to begin a low-level attack, and we would cover them.

Ground radar wouldn't tell us anything about the F-104's, but we knew about when they'd attack. We searched on our radar, but an F-104 is a small plane and a small radar target—we had only a very brief moment, if any, to detect them. They usually climbed to about 50,000 feet and made a descending turn toward our tails, accelerating to nearly Mach 2. We were escorting the F-101's at only about Mach 0.7. The F-104's would often drop just below us and come up below and behind, the "6 o'clock low" attack, closing at high speed. If we didn't see them, their gun cameras would show us just cruising along, fat, dumb, and happy. We were dead!

If we saw the F-104's we'd call 'BREAK" and we'd turn hard into them. The F-104's couldn't follow us in a tight turn, so they'd break off and run for safety. Once I broke into an F-104 and he dove to escape. I dove after him in full afterburner, accelerating rapidly past Mach 1.5 while I locked onto him with my radar. My radar computer showed that he was going away from me at over 200 knots! He got so far below and ahead of me that I couldn't see him, but my radar stayed locked on. Suddenly my radar showed that he was pulling up into an Immelmann half-loop, reversing his direction and coming back to fight. I switched to simulated radar missiles as he zoomed up, cut across his loop and got a "kill". He had made a mistake by trying to return to the fight.

Other times I wasn't so lucky. We had started the inbound attack covering the F-101's and I was looking hard for any radar targets above and ahead of us, where the F-104's would be coming from. I saw a target, quickly locked on it, lit my afterburner and attacked. In less than ten seconds I noticed that I was closing on the target at about 700 knots — which was my own airspeed! My target was not moving — it must be chaff! Impossible! F-104's don't carry chaff! By the time I admitted to myself that I had been suckered off on a bundle of chaff, the air battle had moved on and I had missed the fight.

F-104's were small and fast as greased lightning, but had poor radar and could not turn quickly. This F-104 has external fuel tanks; without the tanks they are hard to see or pick up on radar, but have very limited range. AF Museum photo.

After the mission we all landed back at Tyndall AFB and went into a mass debriefing. Each pilot told what he had seen and done, and his recorded data would be examined. It was hard to put the stories together, and often seemed like we were not even in the same battle. I waited for the F-104 pilots to tell their stories, and none of them mentioned chaff. I could stand it no longer, so I stood up and asked: "OK, which one of you dropped CHAFF"? They all broke out laughing! One of them put a couple of bundles of chaff inside his speed brakes. He kept his speed brakes closed until the moment he thought we'd be in radar range, then briefly popped his speed brakes open and closed. The chaff bundles broke open as they hit the high-speed air, making a cloud of metal-coated fiber needles which I had locked onto. A simple trick, but it worked. It embarrassed me, but showed that an unexpected action by the enemy can gain crucial seconds in an air battle.

Aerodynamics of Combat

As any object accelerates past the speed of sound, the moving shock wave moves the center of pressure (the lift) aft. The faster the plane goes, the farther the center of pressure moves aft. The center of gravity remains in the same spot. As the center of pressure moves aft of the center of gravity, the aircraft becomes nose-heavy. Back trim, or back stick, is necessary to hold the nose up, and that creates more drag as the elevators are raised to provide the needed force. The problem becomes serious during very high speed combat because a nose-heavy aircraft cannot turn as rapidly (not as much "G") as an aircraft which was properly balanced.

There are a number of techniques to overcome the problem of being nose-heavy when supersonic. Some aircraft (F-14, F-111, the B-1) use swing wings to control the center of pressure. Other aircraft (B-70, Concorde air

The F-101 has two engines, good radar and two seats, but could not turn hard. In a high-G turn, its tail could be "blanked out" by turbulence from its wing, causing it to pitch up, lose control, and possibly crash. It was used either as an interceptor or as a photo-recon aircraft. USAF photo.

The Spirit of Attack

liner) use a small wing far forward, called a "canard", which adds extra control close to the nose. The new F-22 has a thrust-vectoring system which can actually change the engine thrust, much like a rocket engine gimbals to guide a large space rocket. The F-106 used a fuel transfer system. When the F-106 accelerated past Mach 1.2, fuel would be transferred automatically from forward fuel tanks to aft fuel tanks. This moved the center of gravity aft to match the center of pressure. The F-104 had no way to counter the center of pressure movement, so the F-106 was able to out-turn the F-104 easily at high speed. Even so, during supersonic combat I often had my control stick all the way back until it jammed against my seat, and I still couldn't get as much turn as I wanted!

A basic concept of aerial combat is the "energy maneuverability egg", which was conceived by the Air Force Academy as they studied the problems of energy maneuverability. Imagine an egg, with the base down. The circumference of the egg at its "equator" is greater than a slice through the upper part of the egg. This egg shape indicates the performance of a fighter: it can turn around faster if it pulls upward as it turns, which is known as "going vertical". Part of this is caused by the force of gravity, which causes you to slow down as you go up, and you can turn quicker when you're slower. You haven't lost the energy as you lose speed—kinetic energy is converted into potential, or stored, energy as you go up and can be converted back into speed or a harder turn as you go back down. If your enemy is turning in a flat circle and you have excess energy, pull up to the top of the "egg" and roll over, tightening your turn and coming back down on him. The bottom of the "egg" is used when you have very little energy left for maneuver and can't go vertical. A high-G turn requires a lot more energy than a low-G turn, and you should save your energy for the moment when you need it most.

The "energy maneuverability egg" is demonstrated in two basic fighter maneuvers: the "High-Speed Yo-Yo" and the "Low-Speed Yo-Yo". You see an enemy fighter crossing in front of you, a few miles away. He sees you, and starts a hard level turn toward you. You both are traveling fast, so you pull up to near vertical, losing speed but turning faster, and drop down on his tail. That was the "Hi-Speed Yo-Yo". In the "Low-Speed Yo-Yo" you're chasing another fighter, both pulling hard G's and you don't have extra energy. Your stick is already far back, so you feed in bottom rudder and drop your nose toward the bottom on the "energy maneuverability egg". As you go down you swap altitude energy for increased speed. Traveling faster and going on the inside of the turn, you cut across the enemy's turn and come up below and behind him. Use your last bit of energy to put your pipper on him and fire guns or missiles! There is a counter to the high—and low-speed yo-yo — do the same thing. If the enemy goes vertical, you must go vertical.

If an enemy is attacking at high speed and is close, you can turn hard into him and force an "overshoot" when he can't match your turn and doesn't have enough distance to execute a high-speed yo-yo. As he passes you, reverse your turn and you're behind him. This tactic is called the "scissors", and uses his excess energy against him. A real scissors usually takes at least two turn reversals before you end up on your opponent's tail. It involves close maneuvering of fighters and has the risk of a mid-air collision, but it can give you an opportunity for a close shot with guns. Most scissors are nearly horizontal, but it is possible to get into a vertical scissors if both planes have plenty of energy.

The "Barrel Roll Attack" is similar to the High-Speed Yo-Yo, when you have plenty of speed and energy and are closer to a head-on attack. You pull up nearly vertical and roll the OPPOSITE to his direction of turn (if he is turning left, you roll right). It's very hard to do correctly, and it can go very wrong. However, when it is done right, it's so beautiful that you can almost hear the victory music playing! I've tried it five times in practice dogfights, and twice it worked out and I felt really good. Three times, I failed and missed the turn so badly that I was embarassed! I learned that the key is to go almost vertical, to the top of the egg, and roll almost inverted to pull down on the enemy.

This book is not about fighter tactics; this is enough to show that energy maneuverability is the key to modern dogfights now that fighters are very heavy and have plenty of power and high speeds. Energy maneuverability probably didn't matter so much in the old days when the speeds were lower and aircraft weights were less significant, but these days you must "go vertical" to win.

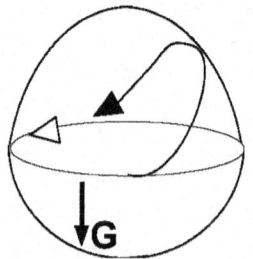

High-speed yo-yo. You have excess energy. Pulling up high and rolling helps cross the "energy maneuverability egg".

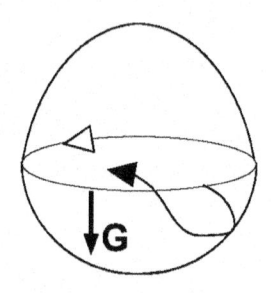

Low-speed yo-yo. Use bottom rudder to cut across the egg and come up from below and behind.

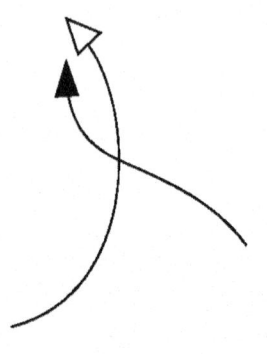

Scissors (horizontal)

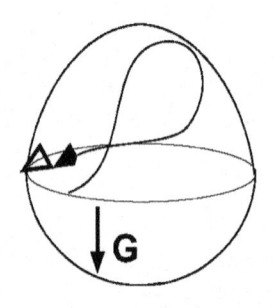

Barrel Roll Attack

Korean Air Defense

The F-106 had great radar and long range. An aerial refueling capability was added, extending its range even further. The F-106's powerful engine and Delta wing (which had more square feet of wing area, and therefore lighter wing loading) were excellent for aerial combat against other fighters. New tactics were needed against fighters. I became an instructor in Aerial Combat Tactics. Soon we were sent to Korea to counter the threat of North Korean MiGs..

From June 4th to November 24th, 1969, I was sent on temporary duty (TDY) to Korea with the 94th FIS, leaving Midge and the kids back at Selfridge AFB, Michigan. The Squadron was at a peak of effectiveness, with everyone trained in radar, infrared, aerial refueling and aerial combat tactics. I was confident of my abilities as a fighter pilot, come what may. Osan Air Base is about 50 miles south of the South Korean capital of Seoul, and only about five minutes flying time from the Demilitarized Zone (DMZ) between North and South Korea. There was a truce in effect, but not peace, so we were ready for war at any time. The North Koreans had more fighters that we had, and the American F-4's and F-105's were largely dedicated to ground attack — leaving our F-106's as the primary air-to-air fighters. Twelve F-106's against a couple of hundred Russian-made MiG 19's and MiG-21's — but our F-106's were better planes and we definitely had the better pilots. South Koreans manned anti-aircraft guns around the field, and guards patrolled everywhere — the North Koreans frequently sent spies and saboteurs to land on South Korea's long shoreline.

From 40,000 feet altitude in the daytime, Korea looks rugged and inhospitable. There seems to be no pattern in the mountains of Korea, and rugged mountains restrict roads from going from the West to East coasts. Looking north over the DMZ into North Korea, the mountains get higher and even more rugged. When flying at night, we could see the powerful searchlights of the South Korean coastal defense forces sweeping across the water, looking for North Korean boats. It's a dangerous place to be.

In the six months that we were there, the North Koreans made two significant landings and five times landed spies (that I knew of). One night a heavy fog rolled in from the ocean and the searchlights created only a bright glow in the fog. A South Korean machine-gun nest on the beach was surprised to see an 8-man rubber raft emerge from the bright fog and paddle right toward their position! When the raft reached shore and North Koreans jumped out to pull the raft ashore, the South Koreans opened fire. The raft was apparently at the end of a rope, because when the shooting started the raft was suddenly snatched from the shore and pulled rapidly out into the foggy darkness — and an unseen warship opened fire with cannon. One of the cannon shells hit about a mile inland, killing a family of Koreans in their home. On a second attempt a month later, the North Koreans landed about a hundred men without being detected. They moved toward an American radar site, but were found by a patrol and were wiped out by South Korean soldiers. South Korean justice is brutal: the officer and top sergeant in the coastal position which had failed to detect the landing were both shot for dereliction of duty.

Korean Mission

The truce which ended the Korean War was often violated. In 1968 alone, 17 U.S. and South Korean military personnel were killed and 294 were injured in 181 incidents. In 1968 the North Koreans had seized the *Pueblo*, a US Navy electronic intelligence (ELINT) ship and imprisoned the crew for a long time. In early1969 they sent jet fighters that shot down a US ELINT propeller-driven RC-121, killing 31 crewmembers. Both the ship and plane had been in international waters, where any nation has a right to go. These were current events when we were deployed to Korea in June 1969. Military personnel overseas have **"Rules of Engagement"** which usually say that you can only shoot in self-defense, after the enemy has fired upon you and showed **"hostile intent"**. Because of the Pueblo and RC-121 incidents, our Rules of Engagement had been modified to state that _the North Koreans had already demonstrated hostile intent_. We could fire upon them without waiting for them to shoot first.

The USA had decided to continue ELINT flights off the coast of North Korea, but now we provided the slow ELINT with a fighter escort. At first we had eight fighters, but reduced it to four fighters. Escort patrol was a long mission; we would refuel in air before starting the patrol. We flew a barrier combat air patrol (BARCAP) about 20 miles off the North Korean coast, and the ELINT aircraft would circle about thirty miles from the coast. Half-way through patrol we would come back to the tanker for more fuel, then resume patrol.

The Spirit of Attack

Two F-106's in alert shelters in Korea. These shelters were built of reinforced concrete. Sliding last doors were later added to stop bomb fragments. We were only five minutes' flying time from North Korea and expected that we would be attacked in the first few minutes of any conflict.

Osan Air Base is out of North Korean artillery range. Their fighters could reach us, and we could reach them. The North Koreans had more fighters than we did, but ours were more advanced.

We flew missions along both coasts of North Korea, staying beyond the 20-mile limit established by international law.

The original North Korean attack drove US forces down to the Pusan Perimeter, which barely held on. A large amphibious invasion at Inchon cut off the North Korean Army in the south. The DMZ was the final truce line, but no "peace" was signed.

My "Korean Mission" story is about events at sea, near Wonson.

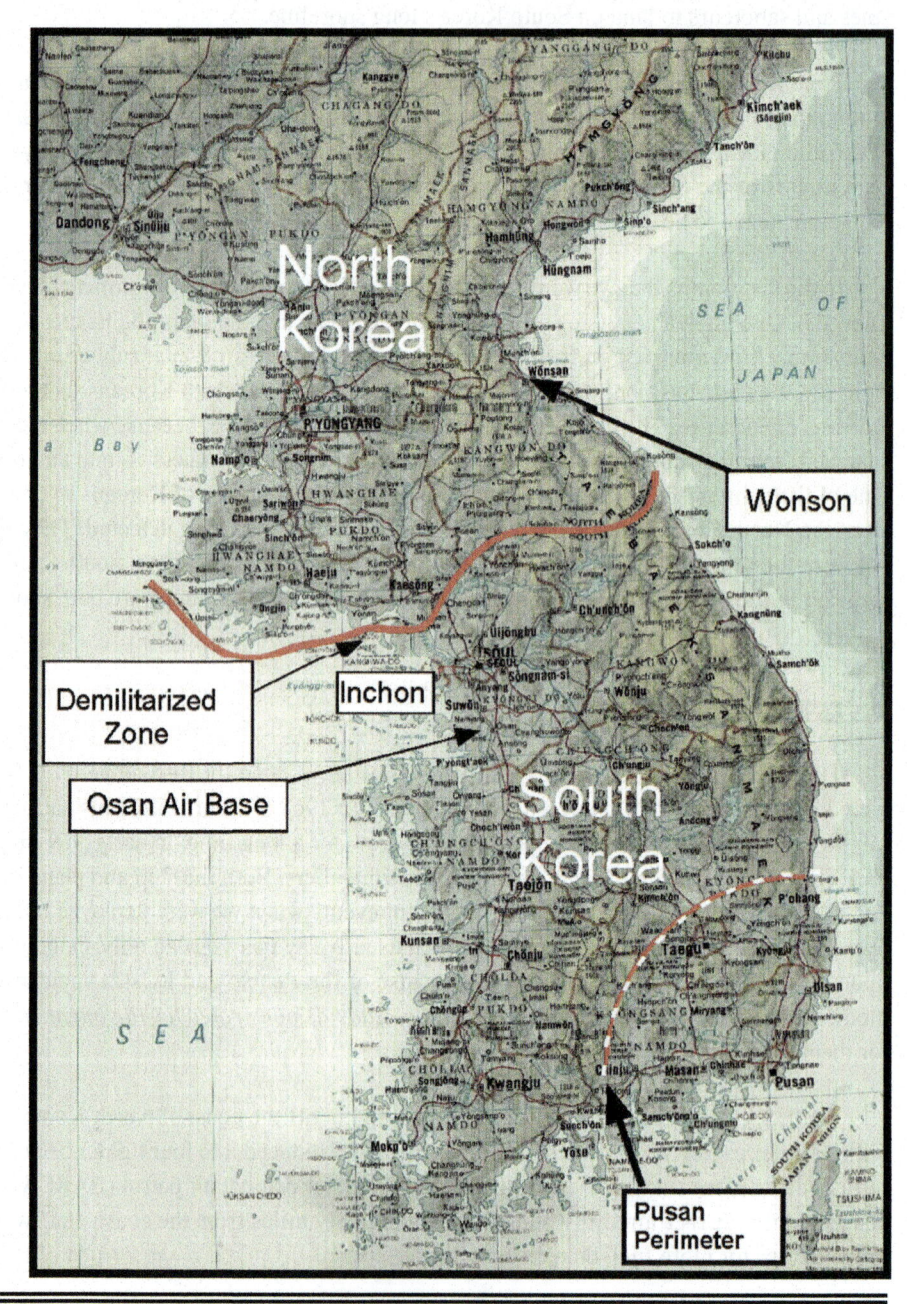

The Spirit of Attack

This mission started normally. Our four F-106's took off from Osan and flew to the east coast of South Korea, where we refueled from a KC-135 tanker. We then turned north to our BARCAP position off the east coast of North Korea, over international waters, sweeping the area with our radar to be sure no fighters sneaked through. The ELINT aircraft was somewhere farther out to sea. We flew BARCAP for an hour or so, then turned south to get another load of fuel from the tanker. I was flying in #3 position in the four-ship flight, with #4 on my wing. #1 and #2 got their fuel from the tanker, and I hooked up to refuel.

"MiGS TAKING OFF FROM WONSON"; our radar station sent a warning that the North Korean fighter base near us was active. I got my fuel, pulled off tanker into a waiting position while #4 slid into position, connected to the tanker, and began to take fuel. "MiGS ORBITING WONSON" came an additional warning. "HOW MANY?" we asked. "ABOUT TWENTY" came the reply. Twenty MiGS against only four F-106's — the odds were interesting — our fighter training didn't cover what to do when seriously outnumbered! A few minutes passed. "MiGS TURNING OUT TOWARDS ELINT AIRCRAFT!" . . ."#4's OFF TANKER". "TANKER TURNING SOUTH". Our last fighter had his fuel, just as the MiGs were coming after our unarmed ELINT aircraft. The unarmed tanker didn't want to be anywhere near the twenty MiGs! Our four fighters turned sharply north and increased to attack speed. I swung into fighting position, my wingman into position on my right wing. The distance between us and the twenty MiGs was decreasing rapidly. They apparently had misjudged their timing — instead of us being low on fuel and south with the tanker, we were full of fuel and closing to attack. The words of the "Rules of Engagement" were in my mind: "*the North Koreans have already demonstrated hostile intent*". Our four fighters armed our missiles — we were attacking! "MiGS TURNING BACK TOWARD LAND". The North Koreans apparently realized that they had missed their opportunity to kill the unarmed ELINT aircraft, and they didn't want to fight. We turned back to our BARCAP area and resumed patrol. My flight suit was sweaty, but the incident was over.

An RC-121 was shot down by North Korean MIGs in 1969 and 31 Americans were killed. This slow reconnaissance aircraft had no chance against MIGs, so we provided fighter escort.
USAF Photo

Overconfidence

SCRAMBLE! In a couple of minutes my wingman and I were airborne from Osan and headed northeast across Korea and then over the Sea of Japan after an unknown aircraft. We climbed to our usual patrol altitude of 41,000 feet and zipped out at about Mach .93. The unknown aircraft was over international waters, so this was just a "look-see" to find out who was snooping around.

We reached the location of the unknown, but there was nothing on radar — until I searched very low and picked up a target. I pulled back the power and opened my speed brakes and started down, with my wingman following in a "fighting wing" position. The target was at least 30,000 feet beneath us and my airspeed increased in spite of my speed brakes. We were closing on the target from above and behind. I locked on with radar and noted that we had a high overtake — the target must be going rather slowly. It was low and slow—what could it be? Then I saw it about four miles ahead and still far below me—and saw that it had four propeller engines.

I rapidly dropped into the 6 o'clock low position where the unknown's pilots couldn't see me, but I was still closing very rapidly and was worried that I might overshoot and go past the target. I recognized it as an Anatov AN-12 transport that we codenamed "Cub".

I had hoped that the target would be something exciting, probably a bomber, like the Bears or Badgers that frequently probed our defenses. This was just a transport, and this would be a very routine intercept. My wingman was holding a good position off to the side—our standard tactic was for one aircraft to provide cover while the other goes in for the intercept. I had done this once before near Alaska as I went in to look at a Russian "Crate" and Ray Janes provided cover (see "It's a Crate" by Ray Janes later in this book). This "Cub" was not flying as low as the Crate had flown, and a four-engine transport was not likely to turn violently. Anyway, I was in his 6 o'clock low position and he couldn't even see me coming.

My power was still back close to idle and my speed brakes were open. I was slowing rapidly enough so that I could synchronize speed with the target just about the moment that I got under his tail. This would be a beautiful join-up with a dumb transport. I'd be sure to get more photos than I got of the Crate! I slid into position just under the transport's tail, very pleased with my flying ability.

AN-12 "Cub" transport. A military intelligence version was modified with tail guns - and I didn't know it!

Russian photo.

I looked up at the tail of this transport from about 100 feet away, and was horrified to see that IT HAD TAIL GUNS, AND THE GUNS WERE POINTED RIGHT AT ME! I was looking right into twin machine gun barrels and could clearly see the gunner looking through his gunsight at me. My heart was in my throat as I broke down and away from those guns. HOW STUPID OF ME! *I could get shot down by a transport!* DUMB, DUMB, DUMB! *Was I to die because I was so stupidly overconfident?*

In seconds I had swung off to the left of the transport to a spot where the tail guns could not point at me. We had intercepted bombers before, but their guns were usually "caged" pointing toward the sky, not pointed at our fighters. This guy had pointed those guns right at my eyeballs from only a few feet away. My heart was beating rapidly with adrenalin as I tried to calmly take photos of this transport. Now I remembered that the "Cub" transport is sometimes used by the NKVD, the Soviet military intelligence unit, and that the NKVD version had been modified to carry a tail gun. There was a photo of one with a gun in our aircraft recognition booklet. This was a military intelligence flight probing our defenses, and the tail gunner probably had not been briefed on the custom of "caging" the guns in a non-threatening position. He had not fired, even though he could not have missed me. Of course, my wingman would have promptly shot him down as blood vengeance. That's what a wingman was for — vengeance, if needed. I took my photos and we went home. I was alive, but feeling stupid.

F-106 vs. F-102

Some F-102's were based north of our Osan air base and we occasionally saw them flying around. I knew the F-102 very well, and knew that it had the same wing area as an F-106. The "Six" weighed much more than the "Deuce" so it had a higher wing loading and couldn't turn as quickly as the "Deuce", but it had a much more powerful engine. I had been an instructor of air combat tactics and had flown both the "Deuce" and the "Six".

One day I was returning to Osan and saw an F-102 flying at moderate altitude. I'm always ready for a rat-race, so I turned toward the F-102 just as he turned sharply to meet me. We passed head-on and the battle was on! I pulled up into a vertical climb, using the power of the Six to leave the Deuce behind. I rolled over at the top of the "energy maneuverability egg" and was surprised to see the Deuce below me, pointed directly at me! I kept up my airspeed and made several passes, but there was no way that I could get behind that Deuce. He was in full afterburner, and walked the plane around on the power of his afterburner, always keeping his nose pointed at me. He couldn't get me, but I couldn't get him, either. I wagged my wings to salute him and flew home to Osan.

F-106 vs. F-4, Low-Speed Dogfight

My wingman and I were scrambled against an unknown aircraft near the east coast of Korea, but the unknown turned around and went back to Russia. My wingman and I cruised back toward Osan. I wanted to check my infrared sight, so told him to lead the flight while I dropped behind to work on my IR systems against his engine exhaust. Suddenly he called out an unknown aircraft which he had on radar about fifteen miles ahead and twenty degrees to our port side. We always took a look at any unknowns. Our wing vs. lead procedures were that the plane with the radar contact knew more than the one with no contact, so I told him to take the "bounce". It was an F-4 headed toward Osan, apparently unaware of our presence as we slid in behind him. My wingman moved ahead of him on the left, but the F-4 crew were daydreaming or something and didn't look around. Finally I pulled up on the right so that the shadow of my plane fell on their cockpit. The pilots looked up in surprise and saw me; a moment later they saw my wingman ahead and to the left. They were in a better position to attack my wingman than to attack me, so they broke left toward him and everyone went to full afterburner.

The F-4 had turned away from me, so it was easy for me to drop right behind and lock on with my infrared tracking. After a couple of hard turns I couldn't see my wingman anymore, and asked him where he was. "Right behind you!" he reported; he had completely out-turned the F-4 and now we were both close behind the F-4. The F-4 pulled into a vertical climb in full afterburner trying to out-climb us, but it was futile. I stayed right behind him, trying various simulated attacks with my infrared missiles. The F-4 finally gave up and turned toward home, wagging his wings for a join-up. We joined him in formation and returned to base, landing without incident. We had proven that the F-106 can easily out-turn the F-4.

F-106 vs. F-4, Low Altitude, High Speed

We had a military exercise in Korea. The F-4's were to carry live bombs and attack targets on the bomb range in central Korea. The F-106's were to defend Korea by intercepting the F-4's while they were over water, headed inbound to Korea. We would not bother them while they were actually firing live weapons on the bomb range.

I wasn't involved in the exercise, but that evening we were in the Officers Club dining room in Osan talking about it. One of our 94th pilots said that he had been directed against an inbound F-4 which was coming in very low over the water and very fast. My friend pushed up the throttle and closed for the attack, coming up behind the F-4 at about a hundred knots closing speed. He got a simulated missile launch and called "MA" (Mission Accomplished) and was starting to break away when the radar controller said "Get his tail number". My friend had almost passed the F-4 at this moment, but he opened his speed brakes to slow down as he turned back and flew close enough to get the F-4's small tail numbers, then zoomed up and headed home.

There was another table at the O. Club dining room which was filled with F-4 pilots who had also been flying that day. One of the F-4 jocks got up and came over to our table. "OK", he said, "We were coming in toward Korea at low altitude, going just as fast as we could, and suddenly an F-106 buzzed us with his speed brakes open! What an insult!"

F-106 vs. F-4, High Altitude, High Speed

SCRAMBLE! In a couple of minutes my wingman and I were airborne from Osan and headed east across the Korean peninsula. We expected to check out unknown aircraft, but this time it was different. "We have a change of call signs for you", the radar controller announced. I had been told that we NEVER change our call signs while airborne because it confused everyone, but the radar controller insisted. Our new call signs indicated that we were #3 and #4 in an F-4 flight. Two F-4's out of a planned flight of four F-4's had aborted, and fighters were needed for a BARCAP mission protecting one of our reconnaissance aircraft (see "Korean Mission" earlier in this story). We were to fly as #3 and #4 in the F-4 flight. We were vectored southeast and soon found a KC-135 tanker which was refueling two F-4's. We dropped in behind and got in line for fuel. As I pulled in to refuel, the boomer said: "You have the right call sign, but you're the wrong kind of aircraft". "No sweat. Just give us fuel", I replied. We topped off with fuel, then turned north with the F-4's.

The F-4 fighter patrol procedures were different than ours—they flew lower and slower. F-106's patrolled at 41,000 feet at .93 Mach, F-4's patrolled at 35,000 feet at .85 Mach. They were leading, so we flew their speeds and their altitudes with them. As we patrolled up and down the east coast of North Korea, we occasionally checked fuel quantities. The F-4's started out with a lot more fuel than the F-106's, but as time went on it was clear that they were using a lot more fuel than we were. We were both carrying external fuel tanks and missiles, ready for air combat, so this was a good test of fuel consumption in combat configuration. Finally the F-4's were running low on fuel, while my wingman and I still had plenty of fuel. We followed them back to the tanker, and we all topped off with fuel and turned back north, resuming BARCAP patrol.

The Spirit of Attack

The Combat Operations Center called, saying that the reconnaissance aircraft had finished its work and we could go home. We joined in close formation briefly, then the F-4 lead called: "Let's go home—FAST"! The F-4's lit their afterburners and entered a gentle dive to gather speed. We lit our afterburners, but held our altitude because I wasn't quite sure what the F-4's were going to do next. The F-4s each had two afterburners, and accelerated faster than we did. We were all going about Mach 1.2 as the F-4s got about a half mile ahead of us and the gap stopped increasing. At about Mach 1.4 it was clear that we were catching them. I pushed the nose down and the two of us rapidly caught up with the F-4s. We were going about Mach 1.5 when we caught them, going about a hundred knots faster than them. We flew right past their cockpits to be sure that our sonic booms would rattle their teeth. Passing them put them in our 6 o'clock position. I didn't want to give them any opportunities to attack us, so I thanked them for the mission and stayed in afterburner as we zoomed up and away. I now knew that the F-4's cruised at 35,000 feet, so I asked radar for cruise home at 45,000 feet—just so I could embarrass the F-4s that fly low and slow!

Four F-106's in echelon formation off the coast of Korea in 1969. These planes have our yellow paint job on the tail, with the Air Defense Command logo. Our "Hat-in-the-Ring" emblem was on the other side of the tail. Between the cockpit and the tail, on the back of the aircraft, is the aerial refueling door where the tanker's refueling probe can be inserted. I was on the ground when my Squadron mates flew this photo op for the Air Force photographer.

F-106's during aerial refueling. The KC-135 tanker has a "boomer", who lies on his stomach in a bulge under the tail. He controls the "wings" on the boom, and guides the boom into the refueling receptacle on the back of the fighter.

The "Hat-in-the-Ring" emblem of the 94th Fighter Interceptor Squadron is visible on the F-106s' tails. I took this photo as I was awaiting my turn to refuel.

The Spirit of Attack

F-106 vs. F-4 "Coco Scramble"

There were three F-4 squadrons on Osan Air Base with us. We were close to North Korea and it was possible that the North Koreans could launch a surprise attack on our airfield. It was critical that we could get our aircraft airborne quickly to avoid being caught on the ground. Getting all the aircraft airborne was called a "Flush". Actually taking off and flying would use a lot of fuel and require full maintenance for aircraft turn-arounds, so Headquarters devised the "Coco Scramble". It was the same as a Practice Flush, but we wouldn't fly. Each fighter would take to the runway, start rolling, light afterburner briefly, then come out of afterburner and taxi back to the parking ramp. This tested how quickly the pilots and ground crews could have gotten the aircraft airborne if they really had to.

The 94th Fighter Interceptor Squadron, with our F-106's, seemed a breed apart from the F-4 jocks. We knew we might have to get off the ground quickly, so our Commander allowed us to buy motorcycle kits (from our own money). We assembled the motorcycles ourselves, and enjoyed riding around the Korean countryside. We parked our motorcycles right beside our barracks. Our ground crews were in barracks which were quite close to our aircraft, while all pilots' barracks were about a mile away. The F-4's had two crew members per aircraft and had three squadrons of aircrews, so they had a lot of men to worry about and used various Government vehicles, mostly extended cab pickup trucks, to move their people. F-4 pilots were in the barracks right beside ours.

We were all still in bed one morning when the base AIR RAID siren wailed. I quickly zipped into my flying suit and ran for my motorcycle. I could hear the base loud speaker blaring: "COCO SCRAMBLE! COCO SCRAMBLE!" As I started my motorcycle, the F-4 jocks were piling out of their barracks and piling into their trucks. One truck was nearly full of pilots, and I heard them shouting: "Where is Joe?" "He's still getting dressed!" "Tell him to hurry"! They were waiting for Joe as my motorcycle roared to life and I headed for our aircraft. There was a golf course between the barracks and the aircraft; our motorcycles roared across the golf course like it was an off-road racecourse. I stopped at our Operations hut briefly, ran in and got my helmet, parachute, clip board and the tail number & location of my aircraft. I jumped back on my motorcycle and raced to my aircraft, dumping my motorcycle in a ditch as I jumped for my plane. The crewchief was already there, the engine intake covers had been removed. The crewchief started the external power unit which provided compressed air to start the engine. In a few seconds my engine was whining up to power, and I gave the signal to pull chocks. I taxied quickly and was the second plane in line, just behind our Squadron Commander. As we pulled to the runway, I noticed that his plane was suddenly slowing down! I pulled past him and saw him waving his hands frantically. I switched radio frequencies to Maintenance, told them the Squadron Commander was having some trouble on the runway, then switched back to Tower frequency, ran up to full power, started rolling, lit my afterburner briefly, came out of afterburner and taxied on down to the far end of the runway and continued back to my parking area. I had to wait to pass by the F-4 area, as their fighters were still starting engines and taxiing out.

There was a big "debriefing" after the Coco Scramble. All of the F-106's had reached the runway before the first of the F-4's! The first F-106 had a problem: the first pilot had hit the throttle with his elbow and had accidentally shut down his engine! Fortunately, Maintenance got the word quickly and had rushed to see what was wrong. Our Squadron Commander had yelled to them to turn a valve in the wheel well so he could use the compressed air stored inside the airplane to start the engine. The crewchief turned the valve and the Commander re-started his engine. In a few seconds his engine was up to full throttle and he released brakes, lit his afterburner briefly, and completed his Coco Scramble. In spite of the accidental shut-down of his engine, he was still able to complete the Coco Scramble before the first F-4 got to the runway! Of course, our Commander had to put up with some ribbing about shutting down his engine with his elbow . . .

Angela Orphanage

I was one of several pilots in our squadron who built Honda 90 motorcycles from kits, and began to explore around Osan. I found a Korean orphanage which needed a lot of help, and soon I was very active with it. There were perhaps a hundred children there, and they were very cheerful — but terribly poor. Their cement block dormitories were very cold in winter, and their meals were cooked in a huge pot over an outdoor fire. They had several children who were good artists, and they knew how to make uniquely Korean lacquered trays with oriental designs such as dragons, flowers, etc. to sell, but they had plenty of competition from other tray makers. I got them to put our 94th emblem, the Hat-in-the-Ring, on the trays. I took the trays onto the base on my motorcycle and sold them to the men in our Squadron, bringing the money back to the orphanage.

I wrote to Midge asking if the people back at Selfridge AFB would help, and they sent a big box of underwear, clothes, and shoes. The skinny, undernourished Korean children were too small for most of the clothes!

Something Big

In the fall of 1969 some strange things occurred which I believe relate to the Cold War, and are not yet known to historians. Our forces in Korea were suddenly put on a high state of alert for "an exercise". In real exercises we fly the planes as much as possible. In this "exercise", we were directed not to fly or even to run engines to check the aircraft systems. Korean nationals were refused entry to our base, so hundreds of Korean workers were kept off the base. Even our normal supply aircraft were cancelled. A strange quiet settled over the base for a week or two, as no aircraft flew and no engines were started. Something big was happening!

The Angella Orphanage in Osan, Korea.

I read the newspapers carefully, and noted that a Japanese reporter said that all the American submarines had left Okinawa — the first time in memory that there were no submarines in port. I saw a newspaper comment that an American aircraft carrier had left Jacksonville, Florida in such a hurry that it left many of its crew on shore, and they were being ferried out to the aircraft carrier somewhere in the Atlantic. Then I got a letter from my wife saying that as she was driving past our home Alert hangars at Selfridge AFB, Michigan, she noted something strange. The hangars had been vacant since we left for our 6-month TDY in Korea, but now there were F-106's from a different squadron, apparently on Alert in our home hangars! That probably meant that our fighter squadrons in the USA had been dispersed to all available bases, so they couldn't be knocked out as easily by missile strikes. Apparently all US military forces were on a heightened state of alert.

Gradually the alert conditions were relaxed. A few aircraft were allowed to fly in much-needed parts, and we could do engine runs to check aircraft. We couldn't fly normal missions, but we could fly active air defense missions. It was early October 1969. I was on Alert, and got a SCRAMBLE order. My wingman and I climbed to 41,000 feet altitude and were vectored northeast, over the Sea of Japan. We flew between North Korea and Vladivostok, Russia. A Russian aircraft was there, but turned back as we came to intercept him (it was over international waters, so anyone had a right to be there).

We turned around to go back to Osan, and I saw a flotilla of warships far beneath me. I knew they were warships because they were much sleeker than cargo ships. I asked for, and received, permission to go down for a look. I left my wingman at high altitude to serve as a radio relay with Korea (we were a long way from Osan) and I dove down to sea level.

There were about seven warships, almost dead in the water – moving just enough to keep control of the ships. A fishing boat was leaving the flotilla at high speed, heading toward North Korea. A FISHING BOAT at HIGH SPEED? Fishing boats don't have powerful engines – yet this one was leaving a wake like a speedboat! I guessed that it must be one of those North Korean warships, disguised as fishing boats, that I had heard of. I was curious, so I first flew to the fishing boat. It suddenly slowed as I flew near it. I couldn't see anyone on deck. I circled for another look, but it now looked like a regular fishing boat.

I next turned toward the fleet. They weren't American ships, so they must be Russian – nobody else would have such a fleet. They had big numbers painted on their bows, so I wrote down the numbers. I had a camera that Intelligence had put in our fighters, so I proceeded to take pictures.

It was international water, so I had a right to be there – but I was careful not to fly in a way that could be seen as threatening to their ships. I got very low over the water, slowed down to minimum safe speed, turned so I would fly through the fleet, and turned on my autopilot. I took pictures as I passed a small ship, then came close to the biggest ship in the fleet – a heavy cruiser – a beautiful ship. Virtually the entire crew was on deck – there were brown uniforms on the lower decks, but the bridge had many white uniforms. I was looking through my camera viewfinder when I saw that the big guns on the ship had been turned on me!

I could understand that very clearly – I was so close that they could easily have shot me down! I turned away immediately and started climbing back to join my wingman. He relayed a message from Osan Air Base: "RETURN TO BASE IMMEDIATELY AND REPORT TO COMMANDER".

I was very excited about what I had seen, and went to the command post promptly. A Colonel was waiting for me, and he was VERY ANGRY. I told him exactly what had happened, and that all my actions followed international law. He said that the Lieutenant who authorized me to go down for a look exceeded his authority. He had me sit down and write up my account of the incident in a report that was to be sent straight to the Pentagon. As he dismissed me, the Colonel angrily said: "Major, you were meddling in something that was MUCH BIGGER THAN YOU!" He ordered me not to talk about it—and I didn't, for thirty years.

Intelligence normally gave us copies of pictures that we took with their cameras (so we could improve our photography) but this time Intelligence said all the photos had been ruined in processing, and I never saw the photos. The "exercise" slowly faded away. I said nothing more to anyone about the incident for twenty years, when I started looking for explanations for what I had seen.

I researched news magazines (TIME and NEWSWEEK) from that time period, and found that Russia and China were having very bad relations. An "incident" on the Amur River boundary between China and Russia resulted in a battle in which many Russians were killed. Reporters said that the Chinese had turned the sewers of Beijing into a defensive tunnel works, with gunports at the storm sewer street drains. I read that the Russians had expelled all the Chinese nuclear scientists, who were studying in Russia, and put them all on a plane headed back to China. The plane crashed, killing the scientists. The Chinese claimed their scientists were murdered. I read an excerpt from a book by one of Richard Nixon's aides which said that the USA had found out that the USSR had decided to attack China before the Chinese could fully develop their nuclear strike capability.

Now it all suddenly made sense! The strange "exercise" that we had, with the submarines sent to sea, the aircraft carriers deployed, and our fighters dispersed to wartime bases – and keeping Koreans off of our bases (it's hard to think of a better way to tell any spies that we're on a war footing!) – this was something that THE RUSSIANS COULD EASILY SEE, BUT WHICH THE AMERICAN PUBLIC WOULD NOT SEE! Our "exercise" was a warning to the Russians, without telling the American people about it.

The flotilla of ships that I saw may have been a summit meeting between Russian commanders and North Koreans. The white uniforms on the bridge of the biggest ship – the whole crew was gathered to honor some VIP from North Korea, and the officers were wearing their dress white uniforms! Perhaps Kim Il Sung himself had been visiting the Russian ship, and was in the "fishing boat" heading back to North Korea after conferring with the Russians about an invasion of China.

As the meeting on the Russian ships concluded, along I came in my fighter plane and buzzed their ships. They would never believe that my appearance was purely by chance, and that I just happened to see them below me and that I was curious. The Russians and North Koreans would conclude that America knew everything about their plans, and that the Pentagon had sent my fighter as a demonstration that we knew what that they were planning, and disapproved.

Since then, I have found a number of records, including declassified National Security Council archives, which confirm that Russia was serioualy planning to attack China but backed off when America indicated it would not tolerate such an attack. I wonder—was my buzzing of the Russian ships taken as one of the "indications" of American resolve? Yes, indeed, I was involved in something big—much bigger than me!

Wake Island

In December 1969 we flew our F-106's back across the Pacific Ocean home to Michigan. I was a Squadron Maintenance Officer, so I was assigned the aircraft which had the most maintenance problems. I carefully selected spare parts which might be needed by our aircraft on the way home, and tied the parts inside my missile bay along with my own luggage. The F-106 missile bay was large enough to carry four guided missiles and a nuclear weapon, so on trips we used it for storage. My friend, Major

The Spirit of Attack

Robert L. Smith, put a whole motorcycle in his missile bay for the trip home! We flew first to Guam for supper and rest. Before dawn the next morning we took off with our tankers and headed for Hawaii, a seven-hour flight. Two hours into the flight my "AC and DC POWER FAILURE" warning lights came on, but emergency power came on quickly and I continued the flight. The AC and DC generators are driven by a rapidly rotating shaft from the jet engine, but they had apparently lost their cooling oil supply. Often the generators would overheat and seize, snapping the drive shaft. This time the shaft did not snap, but continued driving the overheated generators. At first there was only a slight vibration, but the vibration increased to a loud hum which rhythmically rose and fell in pitch. The whole plane began to vibrate with the hum, and I worried that the overheated generators must be red hot and were likely to catch fire. I declared an emergency. I knew that there was a good runway at Wake Island, and I assumed that they had an air/sea rescue team there in case I had to bail out short of land. After another hour of flying with increasing vibrations, we finally saw land. I left the formation and struggled to Wake Island. I got off the runway and shut down the engine as quickly as I could to avoid fire, and took a look in the engine bay. The generators were hot, and the generator shaft had rainbow colors, showing that the metal had been red hot! I had the needed repair parts already in my missile bay, so all I needed was a couple of engine repairmen to fix my plane. A day later, the Squadron sent a transport with two airmen who fixed my aircraft and they then continued on their flight home. I was left alone on Wake Island, trying to schedule a tanker to come by and fly with me to Hawaii.

Wake Island is small, and the runway covers most of the island. The Japanese captured it in WW II, defeating a couple of hundred Marines. Wake has no natural source of fresh water. A large part of the island is covered with concrete to catch rain water and run it into an underground cistern, which was our supply of fresh water. There were few people there—most were Filipino contract workers who provided meals and kept the barracks ready for guests. I was surprised that they had absolutely no air/sea rescue unit—if my plane had caught fire and I had bailed out over water, there was nobody who could have rescued me! Wake had a recreation facility equipped with sports equipment. I swam alone in the lagoon at Wake, enjoying the tropical fish. Once a British Vulcan bomber stopped on its way to Australia, and I had someone to talk to. I went for long walks, finding old Japanese foxholes, pillboxes, guns and bullets. The Japanese landed on the island in the weeks just after Pearl Harbor, and their navy never returned to give their troops aid or supplies. The Japanese dug many trenches and pillboxes while waiting for an American invasion. American ships bypassed Wake, and used it for target practice on their way to the real war in the southwest Pacific. After WW II, the surviving Japanese were returned to Japan. There are memorials on the island to both the American and the Japanese soldiers who died there.

Telephoning home was hard, as the telephones were for official business only.. The Squadron Commander told my wife that I was **"missing over water"**. They had seen me go to Wake and a Squadron maintenance crew had flown to Wake and fixed my plane — why didn't they know where I was? I made many calls to schedule a tanker to come to Wake and take me home. After five days, I finally got a tanker to stop at Wake. The next morning I took off with the tanker and flew in loose formation to Hawaii, landing at Hickam AFB, then on to California, where I left them and flew home. My wife and children were there when I landed at Selfridge—my last flight in the F-106. The 94th was busy moving everything farther north in Michigan to Wurtsmith AFB. I had volunteered to fly fighters in Vietnam, so my orders were to report to Luke AFB in Arizona to check out in the F-100. I was sorry to leave the 94th and sorry to leave the F-106. New adventures awaited.

Wake Island is the only place to land between Guam and Hawaii. Pan American Airways set up a refueling spot for the Pan Am Clipper in 1941. The Japanese captured Wake early in the war. I am exploring a Japanese coastal defense gun. We bombed and shelled the Japanese garrison, but did not attempt to recapture the island. Japanese bunkers and this heavy gun remain as evidence of the war.

Vietnam War

My "Welcome Home" to Selfridge was almost lost in the confusion of events. My wife Midge had been very worried when I was "missing over water" during the five days I was at Wake Island. The 94th FIS had been reassigned from Selfridge AFB to Wurtsmith AFB, farther north in Michigan, and everyone was in process of moving. The Vietnam War was heating up, and I volunteered to fly fighters in Vietnam. If I didn't volunteer, I'd probably go anyway, but in cargo or spotter planes. Five members of our 94th FIS had gone to Vietnam flying F-105 fighters, and only one completed his 100 missions without being shot down. My orders were to go to Luke AFB and learn to fly the F-100 for ground attack missions..

The F-100 was unsophisticated but it had four 20 mm cannon with 1,600 rounds of ammunition (usually high-explosive, incendiary (HEI) and could carry a good load of bombs. It could be very accurate with both guns and bombs if you got close to the target. Our standard 30-degree divebombing attack could hit within 30 feet of the target under range conditions — and a 500-lb bomb made a 30-ft crater. In "high-threat" areas we used a 45-degree dive and released the bomb from 5,000-ft altitude, and our bombing was very inaccurate. My wife and children were able to come to the gunnery range once with me and watch the students firing and dropping practice bombs. It was quite an experience to be in the range tower and watch the fighters strafe the white panel targets.

On June 19, 1970 I graduated from F-100 training, and on June 29th I went to Survival School at Fairchild AFB, Spokane, Washington. I had been to many Survival Schools in my Air Force career, but this one focused on Escape and Evasion techniques. The assumption was that we were shot down in Vietnam and had to hide from Communist soldiers while signaling to rescue aircraft about where to pick us up. Then we had "resistance training" — ways that we could resist interrogation and beatings if we were captured. We learned from the experiences of our prisoners of war during World War II and Korea, including some techniques that are secret even today. The training included several days of semi-starvation and extreme fatigue to prepare us for the physical and psychological problems faced by prisoners of war. This training is a major reason why our POW's in Vietnam were able to survive brutal conditions and beatings, even when held for several years. The training was so realistic that there was a code word: "SCHOOL SOLUTION", which either the "enemy" or the "prisoners" could use to call off any pretense and find the real truth or get medical attention if needed.

Part of resistance training was setting up an Escape Committee, which was secret because our "prisoner" ranks were deliberately penetrated by "informers". My job in the Escape Committee was to arrange a diversion to attract attention away from an escape attempt. I thought that the "enemy" guards had seen just about every diversion tried, and would be hard to fool. I noted that our "prisoner" ranks include one black man with fuzzy Afro hair, and one white guy who looked like a Hitler Youth — a perfect racist! I gathered a tight team for my "diversion" and set up my plan: the black and white guys would hate each other from the very start, and call each other names constantly. When I gave the signal, they would start a fight. The others would join in the fight. We knew that others "outside" the group would all try to break it up, so we could get a real fight going. The fight would be heard by the guys who were to escape; they were to penetrate the barbed wire on the other side of our "prison camp".

The "capture", "interrogation", and "prison" steps went as expected. I secretly passed "escape kits" to the "escapees". My black & white guys (and their supporting cast) got nastier with each other as we spent days in captivity, hungry and tired. Finally the Escape Commander (known as "Big X") gave me the word to start the diversion. I gave the word to my guys, and the fight started. The fight got pretty real, as fists swung — somebody connected a fist with my nose, and my nose bled profusely. I used the blood from my nose to cover my face and

An F-100 on display at Luke AFB, Arizona. Under the wings are fuel tanks; bombs, napalm and rockets also go under the wings. Four 20 mm cannon are under the nose. The big pipe is for aerial refueling.

smear on several others. The fight was so realistic that the "enemy camp commander" didn't know if he had a real race fight or just a fake one; blood was flowing and he had to know, so he called for a "SCHOOL SOLUTION"! The fight stopped immediately and we told him it was just a diversion. During the final "debriefing" of our prison experience, we were told that it was the ONLY TIME in the history of the survival school that the Enemy Camp Commander had called for a SCHOOL SOLUTION! The black and white guys who led it were given a standing ovation by everyone for putting on such a good show. Nobody mentioned that I was the guy who thought it up, or that it was my blood that flowed. An interesting side note is that the fight didn't make enough noise — the "escapees" on the other side of the camp didn't hear it, and did not escape.

At the end of July 1970 I was in top physical shape and weighed 155 pounds, which I now call my "fighting weight". We had a big family reunion at my parents' home in Tucson. Everyone came to see me off to combat in Vietnam. We gathered for a timed photo at lunch near their swimming pool, while the children (aged 2 to 10) played nearby. Suddenly there was a splash, and someone yelled "There's a child in the pool!" I jumped from the table and ran for the pool, diving from a full run with all my clothes on toward a child struggling, face down, in the deep end of the pool. I came up under the child (2-year-old Paul Gordon), lifting and pushing him toward the edge of the pool. My brother Bob was suddenly beside me, taking his son Paul and handing him to my father who was kneeling by the edge to collect the child. It all was over in about a minute, and Paul didn't even swallow any water. My daughter Julie said that Paul didn't fall in the water — he actually ran to the pool and jumped in! This incident shows how rapidly a swimming pool can become a hazard to young children, even with active adult supervision . . .

Jungle Survival School

On August 6, 1970 I left for Vietnam. My first stop was at Clark AFB in the Philippines, where I attended Jungle Survival School, or "snake school". We were trucked into the mountainous jungles of the Philippines where Negrito natives taught us how to eat jungle plants, how to cook rice in bamboo containers, and how to hide in the jungle. Then they paid the Negrito children to go into the jungle near our camp and try to find us; they got a prize for every American they found. My technique was to hide in an unlikely place, so I hid on the face of a cliff in a crevice behind a bush. The children came by, but did not find me. Drinking water is a serious problem for pilots who are evading, and the enemy often hide near creeks or ponds and wait for pilots to come to drink. We carried plastic baby bottles of water in our flight suits so we could go longer without going to a stream for water. We learned to use survival radios and how to be lifted in the sling of a hovering rescue helicopter. After Snake School, I was ready for combat in Vietnam.

Tuy Hoa Air Base, Vietnam

I was assigned to the 309th Tactical Fighter Squadron and flew my first combat missions — it was hard to adjust my bombing from the flat target ranges in Arizona to the mountains of Vietnam, where the target elevation and winds were just a guess. We slept in trailers, which were reasonably comfortable. One night a US Navy cruiser sailed close to shore and bombarded enemy positions, firing its big guns directly over our base. The concussion from the big guns made my trailer pop like a tin can, making the trailer doors swing open every time the Navy fired. I was there barely a month before Tuy Hoa was closed — the beginning of the US withdrawal from Vietnam. The entire base was being abandonned, so we had one last party in the Officers' Club and deliberately tore the place up. The next day I boarded an old C-47 transport and flew down the coast to our base at Phan Rang.

Tuy Hoa Air Base was on the coast of Vietnam, with a beautiful beach. We lived in trailers, two pilots per trailer. The trailers were grouped in rectangles with a sun deck, dart boards, and a bar. There was also an Officers' Club near the beach and a cafeteria for meals. We considered it a rather rustic resort area, calling it "Tuy-Hoa-by-the-Sea".

Phan Rang Air Base, Vietnam

In September 1970 I joined the 612th Tactical Fighter Squadron and soon was involved in daily combat missions. Phan Rang was about five miles from the sea and had a real Vietnamese Communist (Viet Cong) threat. About once a week they would shoot rockets into the base, but they were inaccurate and their aim was poor. One rocket hit the road outside the base laundry and the shrapnel ruined most of our laundry machines. Another rocket hit the front door of the Officers Club, but nobody was injured.

The Viet Cong had trouble with their weapon fuzes. Many times the rockets would not explode when they hit the ground. One night a guard on our defense perimeter reported they were firing at him, but there were no explosions. In the morning there were seven mortar rounds stuck in the soft mud around his position — none had exploded!

Phan Rang was much larger than Tuy Hoa with several squadrons of fighters. Each squadron had its own dormitory or "hooch" with sleeping quarters and a party room. We had a barmaid, "Susie", and four cleaning ladies on our payroll, which was funded by dues charged to the pilots. To supplement dinners at the Officers Club, we frequently grilled nice steaks over charcoal outside our hooch, and I was soon in charge of buying the liquor and the food and paying our Vietnamese workers. The food and liquor came from an Army commissary and was cheap and plentiful. I tried to find out if we were paying our Vietnamese enough

My "Hero Picture" with the F-100 in Vietnam. These were official photos for file -- in case we did something good -- or got killed..

— their pay, converted to dollars at the market rate, was very low. They had had no pay raises in two years, yet Vietnamese inflation was reducing their effective wages. I calculated a new wage which brought them back to their original pay, after figuring inflation. The women were happy — soon every other squadron also raised their employees' wages.

Fire on the Water

January, 1971. Phan Rang Air Base in southeastern Vietnam was settled into the routine of war. We had not had a rocket attack by the Viet Cong in a month, when a rocket had hit near the base laundry and had ruined a couple of washing machines. I was scheduled for night alert this evening, and went to the alert hangar an hour before sunset.

The alert facility was in reinforced-concrete igloo "wonder buildings" strong enough to survive a direct rocket hit. That evening I would be Flight Leader with a young lieutenant flying my wing. My F-100 was loaded with two external fuel tanks, three napalm (jellied gasoline) bombs, and a large parachute flare dispenser. My four 20mm cannon had 1,600 rounds of HEI (high explosive, incendiary) ammunition. I checked the fuzes carefully, set up the cockpit switches and went in for briefing.

My wingman had just been given a night check-out and could now fly night combat missions. I briefed the flight in some detail, and distributed the secret code books that we would use. His aircraft was armed with conventional bombs instead of napalm, so we had a mix of weapons. We had supper and went to bed, fully dressed.

SCRAMBLE! The klaxon horn suddenly blared; I stumbled out of bed, strapped on my G-suit, grabbed my survival vest & gun, and ran for my plane. The crew chief was already there—I scrambled up the ladder into the cockpit, flicked on the battery switch and hit the starter. The engine whined; lights came on—gauges showed increasing fuel flow, oil pressure, and RPM. The crewchief pulled the chocks and I pushed the throttle forward, roaring out of the floodlighted hangar into the black night outside. My wingman was right behind me. There was much to do—the radio crackled with instructions: where to go, what altitude, who to contact, which radio frequencies. I closed the canopy, turned onto the runway, pushed the throttle forward, checked my instruments, released my brakes and lit the afterburner. The red glow of the afterburner flickered as I roared between the runway lights and then up, up into the utter blackness of the night.

My young wingman flew close to my wing as we climbed into a wall of thunderstorms; everything was black except for his aircraft lights and the sudden blazes of lightning. We plunged into the utter blackness of the storm; torrents of rain hit us and the aircraft were tossed in turbulence. A green glow appeared on my canopy; it quickly became fingers of green fire, creeping eerily around the cockpit. Saint Elmo's Fire—static electricity—was a spooky companion in the cockpit. The green fire became so bright that I could barely see my wingman, grimly hanging on to my wing, the green fire dancing and playing with his plane too, as he held tight formation despite the rain, turbulence, and lightning.

Suddenly we broke out of the thunderstorm and into a beautiful, moonless night with stars shining brightly in a clear sky. We flew west, watching the wonders of Vietnam at night. American or South Vietnamese army outposts were encircled by perimeter flood lights; flares and occasional tracers lit one that seemed to be under attack. We flew to our appointed rendezvous and descended to find the Forward Air Controller (FAC) who had called for air support.

The FAC came up on the radio and quickly briefed the situation. Using special night-viewing equipment, he had found three enemy barges unloading supplies on the shores of the Mekong River; the enemy didn't know they had been spotted. We would launch a surprise attack: I would fly directly over them and drop flares; my wingman would attack as soon as the flares lit and revealed the barges. I could make out the river in the starlight, and could see the spot that the FAC described.

"SET E'M UP HOT, ARM NOSE-TAIL, BE SURE YOUR SIGHT'S UNCAGED", I called. My wingman dropped back in trail and prepared to attack. I checked my bomb switches armed HOT, and uncaged my bomb sight. I flew over the spot, guessed at the wind, and pushed a button to fire my flares.

Two flares lit the sky; they floated toward earth on parachutes, lighting the river with a flickering, ghostly light which exposed the barges. The barges were nosed-in to the shore. I bent my plane around in a tight turn to attack; Wing was already diving for the kill! Two sudden flashes on the shore marked the impact of his bombs; then I was diving down, under the flares, and the three barges were in my sights. I punched the bomb button and the plane jumped as a heavy napalm bomb fell away; I "jinked" my plane in violent turns to throw off anti-aircraft fire and climbed back up to start another attack.

The scene below was spectacular. The napalm had hit on the shore, splashing fire on two of the barges. One barge had broken loose from the shore and was drifting downstream, burning and exploding as fuel and ammunition detonated. The other barge burned at its spot on the shore. My wingman was diving for his second attack; his bombs detonated among supplies on the shore, starting a fire which began to grow. I rolled in again, diving toward the fires, and aimed at the supplies that he had uncovered. Two napalm bombs, this time! They hit among the stacked supplies, and the night glowed with billowing flames. Wing was attacking again; his last bombs hit beside the remaining barge and it sank right there. We were out of bombs; I switched to cannon and attacked again to strafe. I dove, put the pipper on the fires and pulled the trigger. My plane shuddered with the recoil of my cannon, and the explosive shells stitched a pattern of sparks in the scene below.

I pulled off the target and watched as Wing made his strafing pass. One barge was sunk near the shore; one was burning, nosed-in to the shore, and the third was drifting down the river, burning and exploding. The fires on the bank told of gasoline drums and ammunition . . .

We thanked the FAC for finding such a marvelous target, and turned home. The FAC's new low-light telescope had denied the enemy the cover of darkness. Years of training and development of new equipment had paid off. Now it was time to go home; the weather was bad—it was time for my young wingman to learn how to get home through bad weather at night. That turned into an adventure that he'll never forget—and a separate story in this book.

The Battle of Prey-Totung

December, 1970. The alert hangar in Phan Rang, South Vietnam, was jolted into action by the blaring of the SCRAMBLE klaxon horn. In a moment, the lounge area was full of running men. I zipped on my survival vest and gun, buckled on my

The Spirit of Attack

My missions from Phan Rang covered most of this map. My biggest single battle was at Prey Totung in Cambodia. I flew over the ancient ruins of Ankor Wat which the Communists used as a supply depot, knowing that we wouldn't attack it. Cam Ranh Bay, just north of Phan Rang, was our major supply center. Phu Cat, north of Tuy Hoa, had F-100's and Marine helicopters. Da Nang, Ubon, and Udon were our primary bases to attack North Vietnam. Nakhom Phanom (we called it "Naked Fanny") was used by Special Forces and helicopters for jungle battles in Laos, or to rescue pilots who had been shot down.

My blue "Party Suit" showed that I was from the 612th Tactical Fighter Squadron. I was a Major and had Senior Pilot wings.

The Vietnam War protesters in the USA had lots of "Peace" symbols, so I wore a "WAR" logo on a chain around my neck.

We wore these "Party Suits" in the evening when we relaxed, and especially if we had a squadron party. There wasn't much to do after flying except drink, eat, and have parties.

Bruce Gordon Stories

The Spirit of Attack

parachute harness, and ran to my plane. My crewchief was waiting as I scrambled up the ladder into the cockpit of my F-100 fighter. I hit the START button and the engine whined into life. Minutes later I was in the air, tucked in formation with my leader, headed for battle.

The lush green mountains of Vietnam seemed to bar our way; our fighters with their heavy bomb loads could barely get through the mountain passes. The scenery was beautiful—a waterfall cascaded into an emerald-green pool in the uplands near Dalat; there were mountain meadows which reminded me of Colorado. A great place to raise crops or cattle—some day, the world may discover this beautiful place in peace . . .

We flew on west, and soon were over Cambodia. The land became flat—miles and miles of scrub brush. We crossed the great Mekong River and started our descent, calling the Forward Air Controller (FAC) on the radio. He directed us toward a Cambodian town and described the situation:

Prey-Totung lies along major north-south roads; a large North Vietnamese Army unit was attacking to the south, along a road. A Cambodian lieutenant was calling the FAC on the radio, telling the FAC where the enemy soldiers were at any given moment. The Cambodian reported heavy fighting on the ground. There was a line of houses on each side of the road; the North Vietnamese had just captured the northern houses and were attacking south.

The FAC circled in his light plane and directed us: "See the barn to the east of the road, near the gully?"—"Roger"—"They've captured that barn. Hit it. You're cleared in HOT!" The lead F-100 attacked, flying a random pattern to confuse enemy gunners, then suddenly diving toward the barn, releasing two 500-pound bombs, then pulling up and maneuvering violently to avoid ground fire. The bombs hit near the barn; as the smoke cleared, the barn was still standing, but was heavily damaged.

The FAC called me: "See the house near the barn?"—"Roger—the white house with the blue shutters?"—"Roger. Enemy troops are in that house—friendly troops are in the next house, just to the south on the same side of the street. Hit the house with blue shutters. Watch out—I see many North Vietnamese troops in the area, and they'll all be shooting at you!"

I circled the area once, planning my attack. I uncaged my bomb sight, selected napalm and armed the switches. The enemy was to the north, the friendlies to the south—I'd attack from west to east, to make it safer for the friendlies—but it put my flight path right along the battle line!

I pushed up the throttle and rolled into the attack, diving and accelerating while twisting and turning to throw off the gunners. There must have been hundreds of them shooting at me. Light smoke from the bushes showed that automatic weapons were filling the air with bullets. I came in at low level, flying straight at the white house with blue shutters. I was at tree-top altitude and flying at high speed as my bomb sight pipper found the target. I pushed the bomb button; the plane lurched as the two napalm bombs dropped and I pulled up over the house, climbing for the safety of altitude. My strike camera (looking behind me) recorded the event: the napalm bombs hit the house squarely, smashing in a wall with their impact; the mass of flaming napalm smashed through the house and flames burst out the windows on the far side.

I circled; my leader was in for his second attack. Then I was back in again, dropping two napalm bombs in a gully near the barn, where enemy soldiers were taking cover. We both went back again, this time with 20mm cannons, shooting up the bushes where anti-aircraft guns were shooting at us. Out of fuel and ammunition, we headed back for our home base—leaving billowing columns of smoke to mark the beginning of the Battle of Prey-Totung.

We got back as fast as we could, re-fueled, re-armed, and struck again. Other fighters joined us; the battle raged nonstop for several days. At night, Prey-Totung was ablaze with tracers and fire; by day, it was a smoking, deadly ruin. Each time I came back, the Cambodians had lost more of the town. We lost contact with the Cambodian lieutenant for a day, and we thought he was dead.

I led the last attack on Prey-Totung, arriving as other fighters were leaving. Smoke from the town could be seen for thirty miles; a FAC was circling, and briefed us on the situation: The Cambodian lieutenant was now trapped in a school on the southeast edge of town. He had over 200 men with him, but only 40 were not wounded. The North Vietnamese had set up an anti-aircraft machinegun on the roof of a large store in the center of town; that gun was giving the FAC a hard time. Our first target would be the gun.

The Spirit of Attack

An armorer installs fuzes on 500-lb bombs at Phan Rang. Half the weight of the bomb was explosive, and the other half was the steel case. The inside of the bomb was deeply cut so that it broke into many pieces of heavy shrapnel when it exploded. The shrapnel was destructive far beyond the blast of the bomb. We frequently installed a 3-foot pipe as a "fuze extender" so the bomb would detonate while still three feet in the air, greatly increasing the shrapnel effect. If we wanted blast, we use a 750-lb "light case" bomb which was mostly explosive.
My photo in the Phan Rang aircraft shelters.

An F-100 loaded with napalm in front of rocket-proof shelters at Phan Rang. A heavy layer of concrete protecting each shelter is visible. The silver containers on the bomb racks under the wings are 800-lb napalm fire bombs. My photo.

Phan Rang in 1971 as seen from the Officers' Club. Some of the aircraft have covered concrete shelters, while others have open revetments which look dark. The buildings in between were our Operations buildings (where we had briefings, planned our attacks and kept our parachutes & helmets) and maintenance buildings. The control tower is easily visible right of center of the photo.

The Spirit of Attack

I armed the switches; I had 500-pound bombs. I decided to play it cautiously against the anti-aircraft gun; I'd bomb from a steep dive, and release at a high altitude—less accurate, but safer. I rolled into a dive, pinpointed the building, and attacked like a deadly meteorite. As I got closer, I saw that the building was a flat-roofed, three-story department store—with a gun on the roof, flashing at me! I released my bombs and pulled out of the dive. The bombs hit in the parking lot—I had missed the target! The anti-aircraft gun kept shooting . . . the gunners stayed with their gun, inviting another attack!

My wingman rolled in—pushing his attack aggressively—he dove right to minimum altitude and sent his bombs right through the roof of the store! The bombs had a slightly delayed-action fuze and blew out the walls of the store, but the roof remained mostly intact. The gun stopped shooting.

We turned our attention to the school where the Cambodian lieutenant was calling for help. The school house was beside a typical oval race track around a soccer field. A large hedge surrounded the entire school area. The lieutenant reported that the North Vietnamese were hiding behind the hedge, shooting the school house full of holes and were ready to attack.

I came in low for a strafing pass with 20mm cannon. I set my sights on the hedge and squeezed the trigger; the aircraft shuddered with the hammering of my cannon. The high-explosive incendiary bullets struck the hedge with a profusion of small explosions, tearing the hedge into a haze of dust and smoke. We attacked again and again. When our bombs and ammunition were gone, we turned for home.

As we left the smoking ruins of Prey-Totung, I thought of the Cambodian lieutenant, surrounded in the school house, with wounded men around him—and the North Vietnamese regrouping to attack. My wingman had a bullet hole in his plane, but we were otherwise untouched. The Cambodian lieutenant was left—perhaps never to be heard from again.

Several weeks later, I was surprised to find a description of the battle in the December 1970 issue of TIME magazine's Far East edition. A French reporter had gone along with some Vietnamese Rangers who landed from helicopters on the outskirts of town, shortly after my last air strike. The Cambodian lieutenant was still holding out in the school house when the South Vietnamese arrived. The North Vietnamese broke and ran away—without a fight—they had had enough! The reporter said the town was completely destroyed, and he saw the bodies of over a thousand North Vietnamese soldiers in the rubble. On the roof of a bombed-out building in the middle of town, he found an anti-aircraft gun. The crew was dead—they had been chained to the gun! This confirmed reports that the North Vietnamese chained or tied their gun crews to the weapons so they could not run away.

The North Vietnamese unit had lost so many men that it retreated up the road to the north, and did not reappear in combat for nearly a year. We had proved again that air power can destroy an enemy force—when we've got troops on the ground who force the enemy to concentrate his forces to attack.

Prey-Totung still haunts my memories, as I fly in at treetop level toward the white house with the blue shutters and send a load of fire crashing through the walls.

Cambodia
The view as I pulled up from a strafing attack on Khmer Rouge troops in the trees above the town. The Khmer Rouge were attacking Government troops holding the road on the dam to top right of the photo. My incindiary bullets have set two buildings on fire. I saw mortar shells exploding in the water.

We refrained from attacking the town itself, which had a large, pretty pagoda in it. The Khmer Rouge (who later exterminated millions on their own people in the Killing Fields) often used pagodas for barracks and storage.

Night Weather

My young winman and I were returning from attacking barges on the Mekong River (see the story FIRE ON THE WATER). The night was beautiful over western Vietnam, but clouds got thick as we headed east toward Phan Rang. I checked the weather: a thick layer of clouds, well above our altitude, extended down to about 8,000 feet and the weather was good under that layer. The clouds would be thick amd it was the middle of the night, but the bases of the clouds were higher than the mountains and there was no other traffic. He was doing a good job as a wingman; it was time to give him real experience leading a flight in weather.

I told him to lead us home, and I moved back onto his wing. We were soon in the clouds and headed toward our initial penetration point (IP). I had the approach chart on my knee clipboard and could glance at it occasionally to keep track of where we were and what we were doing; most of the time I just hung close on his wing and was a good wingman. We were at 20,000 feet and reached our IP, where we should reduce power to 85% and open our speed brakes to begin a rapid descent. He should have nodded his head quickly forward to signal opening the speed brakes, but he didn't nod. Instead, he just reduced power, without speed brakes. I almost called him on the radio to tell him to open his speed brakes, but then I thought: *no, I'll let him make his mistakes—the weather is safe, and he'll learn more.*

We started down without speed brakes. He knew we should be descending rapidly, so he pushed the nose down—but then our airspeed increased far above what it should have been. He decreased the rate of descent to get airspeed under control, but we weren't descending fast enough. I thought he would realize at any moment that his speed brakes were not open, but he didn't notice. Approach Control radar (which could not see our altitude) passed us over to Final Approach radar. Final Approach had precision radar with clear altitude indications, but we were still so high that we were above their radar coverage. Final Approach could not see us at all, and after some confusion passed us back to Approach Control, who could track us easily as we passed right over the field — but still in the clouds, thousands of feet above where we should be. Approach Control turned us on a wide arc to come back for another approach; during that time we descended to our normal altitude. When we switched to Final Approach this time we were in the right place and everything went well.

After we landed, I walked over to him. The night was cool, but his flight suit was wet with sweat. "Do you know where we were? Do you know what went wrong?" I asked. He shook his head weakly. "You forgot to open the speed brakes" I said. We walked slowly back to the debriefing room. He had learned a lot about night weather flying which he would remember for the rest of his life. It had been an emotional night, and we were both very tired.

Low Fuel

The South Vietnamese Army was engaged in a big battle in the northwest corner of South Vietnam, just south of the DMZ. Almost all our targets that day would be in the same area, a long distance from Phan Rang. Thick clouds and rain moved in the night before, and a wet fog kept us grounded all morning. Finally the clouds lifted enough to allow operations and all pilots went to their planes. Instead of taking off at the usual 20-minute intervals, we were lined up for takeoff like airliners at a busy airport. We took off in flights about three minutes after each other, and all flew to the same area to attack. We circled while the FACs marked targets, dropped our bombs, and headed home. We had all gone the same long distance, and we were all low on fuel when we approached Phan Rang.

My wingman was tucked in nicely beside my wing, and by hand signals I asked how much fuel he had. Both of us were low on fuel, and needed to land without delay. We were flying above a thick layer of clouds as I contacted Phan Rang Approach Control, declared low fuel, and asked for an expedited approach to the field. Approach Control said there would be a 35-minute delay because of all the airplanes stacked up, and that they <u>all</u> had low fuel! We didn't have enough fuel to wait 35 minutes.

I rechecked the weather, and all bases in South Vietnam had marginal weather. I could go to Cam Ranh Bay, but our F-100s were needed at Phan Rang for the next day's missions. Phan Rang was on the southeast coast with a horseshoe of mountains and a big opening leading to the ocean. The weather at Phan Rang was not bad—about 4,000 feet ceiling and 5 miles visibility. The problem was the thick layer of clouds and the many airplanes in holding patterns waiting for their approach times. I could hear many flights calling in low on fuel, and more were coming. Approach Control couldn't handle all the fighters with low fuel.

Something had to be done, quickly. We were all flying on Instrument Flight Rules (IFR) which put us in the stack of fighters waiting for approach times. They were orbiting at various altitudes in the "stack". Hand signals confirmed that my wingman was lower on fuel than I was. We had to either go down now, or go to Cam Ranh Bay. I called Approach Control: "CANCEL MY IFR. I'LL GO IN VFR". Approach Control sounded incredulous as he acknowledged my call. I was going in visually! I was taking a big risk and violating regulations, but I wanted to get our two plane back to base quickly so they could rearm for the next mission. Maybe it was the Spirit of Attack . . .

I turned out to sea and flew long enough to have crossed the mountainous coast and be over water. My wingman held tightly to my wing as I started a quick descent into the clouds, violating the VFR regulations. The clouds seemed endless as we descended toward the water. I was nervous about violating regulations but I needed to get our planes on the ground quickly. Finally we broke out under the clouds, with water under us, and we turned back through the opening in the mountains to our base at Phan Rang. Flying visually, it was easy to fit our two aircraft in the slow line of instrument approaches. In a few minutes, my wingman and I were on the ground taxiing to park our planes.

I waited with dread to be called in for violating regulations, but the call did not come. Instead, I heard that a number of other flights had heard my call to cancel IFR, and they had done the same thing. Those flights which followed me helped reduce the IFR traffic congestion so the rest could come in normally. I heard that there were staff meetings called to discuss the situation, to be sure that they never again had so many airplanes up there with low fuel at the same time. Maybe I should have got a commendation for canceling IFR, but at least they didn't give me a reprimand.

Enemy Fire

I picked up my mail from the Phan Rang post office and wandered back to my barracks, reading the news from home. Suddenly there was an explosion behind me, and the sirens wailed "TAKE COVER". The sirens always sounded AFTER rockets hit! I ran to my barracks and grabbed my camera—I wanted to get photos of a real rocket attack! I climbed to a high spot and looked out over the base. There were a number of other idiots, besides myself, standing on high spots with cameras in hand. Our Vietnamese cleaning girls were all in our bomb shelter, waving at me to come in where it was safe. We usually got hit with only one or two rockets per week, so I wasn't worried. There were no more rockets and the "ALL CLEAR" sounded, so I went back to see what the rocket had hit. It had hit in the road between the post office and the base laundry. A sergeant driving a truck had seen the rocket coming; he jumped out of his truck while it was still moving and broke his leg; he was the only casualty. The rocket made only a shallow crater in the road, but the shrapnel went in all directions. I went in the base laundry and saw that the shrapnel had made holes in several washing machines. That night, I came back and stood in the rocket crater and was fascinated to look at the building around me and see all the little lights where the shrapnel had punched holes in the buildings and the interior lighting was making little light beams heading right back to the spot where I was standing. I made a mental note that the shrapnel from a rocket is much more dangerous than the primary blast.

A week or so later, it was a cold, rainy night. The base siren wailed "TAKE COVER", then "ALL CLEAR", then "TAKE COVER", then "ALL CLEAR" again. This repeated for several hours; I just put on my body armor and went back to bed. There were no explosions. Later I heard the story:

One of our guards in a watchtower heard something go "thump" at the base of the tower, and set off the alarm. Nothing happened, so they blew "ALL CLEAR". He heard more "thumps" and was sure someone was shooting at him, but there were no explosions. He spent a very worried night. When dawn came, he looked around and found seven enemy mortar shells stuck in the mud around his guardpost! Their ammunition had got wet, or the mud was too soft to set off the fuzes. Several other times there were rocket attacks but the enemy rockets did not explode. One did explode and blew in the door of our Officers Club but nobody was injured and we fixed the door quickly. Enemy fire didn't hit anything more important than the washing machines in the laundry while I was a Phan Rang.

The story got back to us that one morning there was a shift change at a guard tower. The new guard approached and called out, but there was only a muffled cry from the tower. Fearing that something terrible was wrong, the new guard called for backup and cautiously approached the tower. He could hear the guard whimpering above, so the new guard carefully climbed the ladder into the guard tower. A large snake had climbed into the tower, and the guard was cowering in a corner, too terrified to move! The guard had many weapons, but a man who is really afraid of snakes is not logical!

Friendly Fire

I was in my barracks writing a letter home when there were three heavy explosions and the siren wailed. The explosions were down by the flight line, so I was worried that our planes might have been damaged. As soon as the "ALL CLEAR" sounded, I went down for a look. There were craters right near our bomb dump. I later heard that a US Army artillery unit had got the wrong target coordinates and nearly hit our bomb dump!

We were launching aircraft one morning when there was a small explosion beside the runway. We all took cover but nothing else happened, so we continued with work while an Explosive Ordnance Disposal (EOD) sergeant went out in a truck to see what had been shot at us. There was another small explosion, and an ambulance was sent out to the scene. A day later I talked to our Flight Surgeon who was in the ambulance and heard this story:

The fighters taking off that morning were carrying CBU-42. These Cluster Bomb Units were small aerial mines, the size of a hand grenade, packed several hundred in a large dispenser hung like a bomb on the fighter. When the pilot pushed the bomb button, the CBU-42 would fall out of the dispenser in a stream of bomblets. After the bomblet hit the ground it would wait several minutes to stop rolling, then springs would throw out some weights with thin fishing line attached. The clear fish line would hang in the bushes for a few minutes, then the mine would arm itself. If anything touched the fishing line it would set off the small mine. We used to drop thousands of these along the Ho Chi Minh Trail to stop the troops and people who came down the jungle trails carrying supplies for the enemy.

This morning, a few bomblets had fallen off a fighter as it took off and nobody noticed. The bomblets bounced along the runway and into the tall grass beside the runway. The bomblets threw out their fishing lines and armed themselves. Maybe an animal touched the fishing line, as one bomblet exploded. The EOD sergeant went out to look, and tripped one of the fishing lines. The exploding bomblet put shrapnel in his leg, and he went down, calling on his radio for help. The ambulance came rushing up and our flight surgeon ran to the side of the wounded man. *"Doc, I saw it. It was CBU-42. There must be more of them all around us"*. The Doc looked around with worry and asked, *"How do we get out of here?"* The wounded man replied: *"JUST EXACTLY THE WAY YOU CAME IN"*! They got out OK.

One of my friends was a Forward Air Controller (FAC) flying a light observation plane and told me his "friendly fire" story: He was at a forward Army base which used flare pots as runway markers. He slept in a tent close to his light plane. The weather was bad so he went to sleep early. An Army artillery unit moved in as he slept, and the flare pots were in the way of their trucks, so they moved the flare pots. He tried to sleep during the roar of trucks driving by his tent and lots of men talking, but was woken up in the middle of the night as they started firing their artillery from positions along the runway, not far away. Then his SCRAMBLE phone rang: American troops are taking enemy fire! Take off immediately and find who's shooting at them! He stumbled out of his tent and saw that it was so foggy that he could barely see the flare pots, but he'd take off anyway and perhaps land someplace else that wasn't foggy. He lined up his plane with the flare pots and started his takeoff roll. He was just lifting off the ground when his plane hit an Army tent; he went through the tent and crashed into an artillery piece just beyond, scattering the troops in all directions but nobody was hurt. His plane was wrecked, so he stumbled back to his tent. The SCRAMBLE line was ringing again—they told him to cancel the scramble because the American troops were no longer getting hit with artillery fire. Later, they found out that the artillery battery that he had crashed into was the one which was accidentally firing on American positions. His attempted takeoff in the fog with misaligned flare pots had knocked out the gun and had saved the American troops!

Inflight Refueling

I had done inflight refueling in Alaska and Korea with the F-106, which refueled easily from a tanker's boom. The boomer controller in the tanker would guide the boom to poke into the F-106 just behind the cockpit, and the boom would lock into position. All the pilot had to do was stay in close formation just below and behind the tanker. The F-100 in Vietnam had a long probe that came from the right wing root and poked an ugly pipe up forward of the pilot's head (see the photo above). The tanker would hang a basket of wire and metal strips on the end of its boom, and it was up to the fighter pilot to stick the long pipe into the basket.

The damn basket was on a short rubber hose and would spin and weave in all directions. It was tempting to try to look to your right and try to stick the probe into the basket, but it caused vertigo. If you banked slightly to the right to get the basket, the probe would go down before it went right, and you'd miss the basket. The best technique was to focus on the "knuckle" where the solid boom was joined to the rubber hose to the basket. This was just a bit above and forward of the basket. I would fly so that the "knuckle" was about six feet ahead of me and six feet to my right, and hope that the probe went into the basket.

Arming the guns and bombs before takeoff. The pilot puts his hands above the instrument panel, away from any switches, while the armament man removes the safety pins from the bombs and loads the first 20mm cannon shells into the guns. From then on, the guns shoot when the pilot pulls the trigger. We carried 1,600 rounds of 20 mm cannon. The big tank in the foreground is a 230-gallon external fuel tank. The slimmer object is a 500-lb bomb (we carried four or six); the small arming propeller is visible. The long pipe is for inflight refueling. This pilot was killed in combat a few weeks later.
My photo.

Once the probe was in the basket, refueling began, and new troubles arose. As the F-100 took on fuel, it got heavier. An F-100 with a full bomb load and nearly full of fuel took 100% power to keep up with the tanker. If you got especially heavy or were at a higher altitude, even 100% throttle wasn't enough and you'd have to use intermittent afterburner just to stay up with the tanker! Rather than use afterburner, you could call the tanker with the word: TOBOGGAN. The tanker would pull back power and start a gentle dive; you'd get extra airspeed from the descent and could keep your probe in the basket, getting fuel. The basket didn't lock onto your plane like the solid boom did with the F-106 and other fighters. If you didn't keep up, the probe came out of the basket; if you overran the knuckle the rubber hose would break off; nobody else could refuel from that tanker and you could come home with a basket hanging on your probe. Most embarrassing!

Aerial refueling was needed to get our planes from Phan Rang, in southeast Vietnam, to places like Tchepone, in Laos. Tchepone was a road junction and small hamlet just to the west of North Vietnam, and was a key point on the Ho Chi Minh supply trail. A road junction makes a good interdiction target, so we bombed it often. The North Vietnamese put up lots of anti-aircraft guns in and around Tchepone,. A mission to Tchepone was long, starting with air refueling and a long flight north over hostile mountains. When we got to Tchepone, there was always a FAC in an observation plane who would shoot a smoke rocket to pinpoint the target for us. We'd roll into a steep dive and the antiaircraft guns would start shooting. By the time we dove to bomb release altitude the antiaircraft bullets were all around us. Pickle off the bombs and start to pull out — but you're still going down for a few thousand feet more. The gunner know that the bottom of your dive will be almost directly over the target, so they pour their fire at that spot. You haul back on the stick and pulling heavy G's, with antiaircraft to left, right, and ahead of you. You "jink" with random, hard turns to confuse the gunners, and struggle back to the safety of altitude. I recorded a tape of one of our fighter songs; it concludes: "Oh, don't go to Tchepone!

Bomb Fuzes

Fuzes seem like simple things, but they're not. A proper military explosive has to be safe to handle until the moment you want it to explode. A bomb is amazingly shock-resistant; a railroad train with a full load of bombs derailed in Arizona, scattering bombs all over, but none exploded. If the pilot forgot to arm the fuze, he could drop a bomb from high altitude onto concrete and it would not explode.

Bombs are shipped and loaded onto the fighters without fuzes. An armorer would insert fuzes into the nose and tail of the bombs. There is a simple brass propeller on the nose of the fuze. This propeller turns in the wind and counts the times the propeller has turned, so that the time to arm the fuze can be set. The armorer installs a wire that pokes through the fuze propeller and keeps the propeller from turning. The other end of that arming wire goes to the fighter, to an electrical solenoid clamp, which is in turn controlled by the arming switch in the cockpit. When the pilot flips the "ARM" switch, the solenoid clamps on the wire and holds it tightly. When the bomb is dropped, the airplane holds onto the wire and pulls it out of the bomb fuze. The brass propeller can turn freely in the wind, and the spinning propeller arms the bomb. The time to arm was set by a dial on the fuze.

When you drop a bunch of bombs together, they could bump into each other on the way down and the resulting explosion could destroy your plane. We normally set the fuze times so the fuzes wouldn't arm for four seconds after the bomb was dropped, a safe distance from the fighter. If you wanted to drop bombs from low altitude, though (such as in a "Troops in Contact" situation) four seconds was too long—the bombs would hit the ground before the fuzes armed and would not explode. For those cases we set the fuzes to two seconds arming, and had to find a way to get the bombs far enough from the fighter in those two seconds. We used "high drag" bombs for low altitude attacks. These had strong metal fins attached to the tail of the bomb. When the bomb was released and pulled the arming wire, the fins opened like flower petals to catch the wind and slow the bomb down. By the time the bomb hit the ground, the fighter was a safe distance ahead. Even so, low-altitude bombing with large bombs was dangerous. I often could feel the shock wave from the explosion of my own bombs. I knew that there was shrapnel from my bombs traveling with that shock wave, and was fortunate that I never got hit by pieces of my own bombs. One of my friends dropped bombs during the Battle of Prey Totung and got hit by his own shrapnel. His plane caught fire and he was able to get far enough from the battle so there were no enemy troops where he bailed out. We circled above him for a while until a helicopter picked him up safely.

Another feature of fuzes was a delay between impact and explosion. If you were after surface targets, you set the fuze for instantaneous explosion. If you were after bunkers or other deep targets, you set the fuze to .025 seconds delay. That gave the bomb time to get about thirty feet under ground before it exploded.

A weakness with our fuzes was that they were timers and could not measure their height over the target. Radar proximity fuzes (used in anti-aircraft shells) were expensive and probably wouldn't work at the long ranges needed for bomb fuzes—a thousand feet or more. A strategic bomber could use timed fuzes because the bomber flew level at a planned altitude and he knew the exact elevation of his target above sea level. A fighter would be diving down at a high speed, so release altitude could be anywhere in several thousands of feet. The fighter, too, would be after targets in hills or mountains where the target could be anywhere in the hills or valleys.

This weakness was especially apparent when we dropped CBU-24. This was a bomb filled with bomblets the size of a hand grenade. If the fighter dropped the bomb at the right altitude, the CBU case would open a thousand feet above the target, scattering hundreds of hand grenade bomblets over an area the size of a football field. CBU-24 was especially effective against anti-aircraft guns, which had to be open to the sky and we could drop bomblets right into the gun pit. If you dropped the bomb too low, it would hit the ground before the case was opened and it was ineffective unless you actually hit the gun pit, which was unlikely. On the other hand, if you dropped the CBU-24 too high, the case opened too high and the bomblets spread out in a "donut" pattern. The hole of the donut was where your target was — you put bomblets all around the target, but none would hit the target! I saw that happen several times.

The Spirit of Attack

Thanh Hoa Bridge

This railroad bridge in North Vietnam was an example of the limitations of our fuzing and weapons during the Vietnam War. It's name means "Dragon's Jaw" and it killed many of our men. I did not personally attack it, but read the reports. The bridge was designed by French engineers and looked like a smaller version of the Golden Gate Bridge in San Francisco. The railroad ran across wooden ties in the floor of the bridge, while towers and cables suspended the bridge over a river. It was very important for North Vietnamese supplies flowing south, as they crossed this bridge before they got to the Ho Chi Minh Trail. Downing this bridge would seriously hurt the North Vietnamese invasion of the south. The North Vietnamese put lots of anti-aircraft guns and even SAM missiles near the bridge to guard it.

Our first attack on the bridge was a failure. F-105 fighters flew at high altitude to stay out of the anti-aircraft fire while they found the bridge and circled prior to attack. Suddenly a MiG fighter popped out of a cloud bank and shot down a bomb-laden F-105, then ducked back into the clouds and was gone. The other fighters dropped their bombs at the bridge; the strike photos were impressive, but the bridge was undamaged. We flew more strikes against the bridge — about 500 air strikes against this one bridge! The steel bridge was anchored into massive reinforced abutments. 500-lb bombs would explode without destroying it. Larger bombs meant fewer bombs per aircraft, and the bomb fuzing had to be just right for the part of the bridge it hit. If you aimed for the concrete bridge abutments you set a delay for the bomb to penetrate the concrete before exploding—but if you hit the main part of the bridge instead, the bomb would go right through the wooden planking and explode in the air under the bridge, doing little damage. If you targeted the steel parts of the bridge, you set the fuze to instantaneous—but if you hit the concrete abutments instead, the bomb exploded on the outside doing little damage. Dive-bombing the bridge was extremely hazardous, with MiG fighters popping out of clouds and heavy anti-aircraft fire as you tried to place your bombs on target. A mission against Than Hoa took lots of planes—not just fighter-bombers, but aerial refueling, fighter escorts to battle the MiGs, and "Iron Hand" strikes that hit the anti-aircraft guns with CBU-24. The enemy added SAM anti-aircraft missiles, so we added "Wild Weasel" fighters to attack the SAMs. We damaged the bridge time and again, but the North Vietnamese quickly repaired it.

Then we got a new weapon: laser-guided bombs. They were not as sophisticated as modern laser-guided bombs, but were a huge improvement. One F-4 fighter circled the target while his back-seater focused a laser on the bridge abutment by aiming a rifle scope. A second fighter dove at the abutment, dropping two large 2,000-lb guided bombs. The bombs hit the abutment, their fuzing was correct; the blast destroyed the abutment and dropped the bridge into the water. Two planes with a new weapon had broken the Dragon's Jaw after 500 earlier sorties had failed. A new age of precision was upon us!

The F-4 Phantom carried a very heavy load of bombs and had a 20mm cannon. It was big, ugly and guzzled fuel, but had plenty of engine power. The F-4's famous Gatling gun fired 6,000 rounds per minute, the same rate as the F-100's four 20mm guns. The F-100 could maneuver better and could be closer to the target at bomb release than the F-4. Closer to the target meant better accuracy, both with bombs and guns. The F-100 was the preferred fighter for close support of ground troops. Later in the Vietnam War, laser-guided bombs gave the F-4 the accuracy that it needed to hit pinpoint targets. USAF photo.

The Dog's Head

A typical target was the Dog's Head in Laos. It was one of many "interdiction points" where the maze of roads known as the Ho Chi Minh Trail was forced by geography into narrow crossing points. Our strategy was to make the roads impassible and thus choke off the flow of supplies to the Communists in the south. The enemy responded by defending these points with many antiaircraft guns. We estimated that they had 1,500 antiaircraft guns and over a thousand trucks on the Trail. They hid bulldozers near the interdiction points to repair the damage to the roads promptly after our attacks. The interdiction point strategy was a failure — it would have been much more effective to attack the ships and docks of Haiphong harbor in North Vietnam, or mine the waters of North Vietnam — but that was not politically acceptable because the ships belonged to Russia and China. Photos of Haiphong showed hundreds of trucks and piles of supplies waiting for the trip south — and we were ordered not to attack them.

The order to attack an interdiction point like the Dog's Head would come on a Fragmentary Order, or "Frag", from 7th Air Force Headquarters in Saigon. The Frag said which squadron would launch how many planes at what time, what our target was and what our armament would be. The missions were spread through the day and night to allow a constant cycle of takeoffs, landings, refueling and maintenance. Sometimes I walked down to the briefing room when the stars were still in the sky and the morning air was cold. We usually flew in pairs; I was usually the flight lead and briefed my wingman on procedures. I was a 36 year-old Major, and my wingman was usually a young Lieutenant or Captain — they had the "spirit of attack" but sometimes made serious mistakes.

After briefing, we would "sanitize" ourselves by removing everything personal except our Geneva Convention identification cards and some money. Bad experience had shown that if you were shot down and captured, any personal information could be used by interrogators against you. A simple thing like your military shot record contained an effective list of the bases you had been assigned to, and told a lot about your training. The Geneva Convention card carried our name, rank, and serial number — which the Geneva Convention on treatment of prisoners of war said that we must give to our captors. If we didn't have such a card, they could consider us spies. After sanitizing ourselves we would pick up our helmets, parachutes, and pistols, and walk to the planes.

Our preflight inspection of our aircraft included a good look at the bombs we would carry. On the nose of each bomb was a fuze with a little propeller; a simple arming wire kept the propeller from turning until we dropped the bomb. As we dropped the bomb, the wire would pull out and the propeller would turn in the wind, arming the bomb. The fuze also had a timer — if we were attacking surface targets (like troops) we set it to zero delay. If we wanted the bomb to go deep in the ground before exploding, we set the fuze to a .025 second delay. Sometimes we set delays of several hours, so we might catch bulldozers which were always repairing the roads.

I was often ready a few minutes early, and would talk to my crewchief and wonder if I was going to be killed in the next hour. There was a poem that sometimes ran through my head, called "An Hour Before I Fly". I thought of Midge and the kids. Then it was time to climb into the cockpit and start the engine.

From the moment the engine started, all was business. We taxied to the arming area where the last safety devices were removed. On the runway, I'd run up the engine, look at my wingman to be sure he was ready, then release brakes and start the takeoff roll. Even with afterburner, the planes were heavy and gained speed slowly, barely getting off the ground. There was a hill ahead of us, and we could barely get over it. We'd climb to about 20,000 feet altitude and navigate to the target area, where we descended to 10,000 feet to see the target better. There was usually a Forward Air Controller (FAC) in a light plane. We'd check in, telling what weapons we had on board, and he'd tell us what he guessed the winds were. He would usually fire a smoke rocket near the target, and would tell how many meters from his smoke to drop our bombs. We'd circle to be sure of the target, and start a dive; the wingman was about twenty seconds later, so he wouldn't be caught by our bomb blast.

Antiaircraft bullets travel about 1,000 feet per second, so at 10,000 feet it took ten seconds for a bullet to get to our altitude and even mild weaving meant they couldn't hit us. As we dove, the situation changed rapidly — we dropped our bombs at about 3,000 feet and completed our pullout about 1,000 feet — bullets took only one second to hit us. Low-level strafe was at 50 feet, where even rifles and pistols could hit us. Our pullout was almost directly above the target — the moment of greatest danger. We'd "jink" hard — sudden, random turns to throw off the gunners — and climb rapidly back to safety. We'd check each other for bullet holes, and would fly home for a drink at the bar.

The Spirit of Attack

Troops in Contact

The most dangerous mission was "Troops in Contact", where friendly soldiers were actively fighting. We had to be very accurate, so as not to hit our own troops, so we would attack at only 50 feet above the ground — where even rifle fire could hit us. We carried high-drag bombs (which had a parachute-like device on the bomb to slow it down and let us get away from the bomb blast) and napalm "Nape", which rolled fire across a football-field area and was deadly against troops. Then we'd come back at low level and strafe with our 20 millimeter cannon, "20 Mike-Mike". The poem on the next page describes our feelings.

The Dog's Head in Laos on a clear day. This was a major interdiction point where the Ho Chi Minh Trail crossed the Mekong River. Two "underwater bridges" are visible - at the dog's eyebrow and at the back of his neck - rocks piled in the river make it shallow for a truck to cross. Later the underwater bridges were repalaced with pontoon bridges that could be quickly repaired. Long lines of bomb craters are from B-52 bomber strikes. Fighters make single craters.

My bombs, and my wingman's bombs, explode near the Dog's Head. The white smoke shows that we dropped Clustered Bomb Units (CBU), which were several hundred grenade-size bomblets in a light case. The case split open as it fell, and the bomblets fell over a wide area. CBU was effective against trucks and antiaircraft guns, which had no roof and the bomblets fall inside the gun pit. This time we were after antiaircraft guns.

Bruce Gordon Stories

Poem—"An Hour before I Fly"

The following poem is on a plaque in my home today. It was written by a Forward Air Controller (FAC) and tells of putting an air strike on the Communists (called "Charlie" or the "Gooks"). It can be sung to the tune of the "Wabash Cannonball". I thought of it many times as I waited to start engines and go on a mission:

As I sit here wondering, just how it will be
Today when flying up on high, feeling quite alone and free
Will I hear those fateful words, "Troops in contact, Sir,
The Army's in a jam again, and they need our help, you see"

"Pinpoint, please, the target", the grunts are pleading now,
"They're hitting us with everything, there's nothing we can do
If you see ol' Charlie, a-hiding in the trees,
When the jets come screaming down, much action you will see."

The fighters soon are overhead, with eagerness they fly,
Their skills are polished to the hilt, they too don't want to die.
"Just mark for us the target, and we will do our best,
To hit your smoke consistently, and lay Charlie to his rest."

"High drags, Nape, and 20 Mike-Mike, is what you have for me.
This makes me very happy, for what a show they'll see.
The friendlies' mark is to the East, the Gooks are to the West.
My mark's away, my smoke is good, I'll let you do the rest."

"Set 'em up HOT, arm nose-tail, make sure your sight's uncaged.
I'm turning base, I have your mark, I have the FAC in sight."
"OK, lead, you're looking good, you're cleared in hot today.
So come on down and pickle . . . Roger, two away."

Number two comes right behind, and does his level best,
To put his bombs on target; he too has passed the test.
"Now hold high and dry a moment, till the smoke has cleared away
For I must get a closer look, to give a BDA."

"This is the Ground Commander, your boys were good today.
The shooting's stopped, the smoke has cleared, I'm sure they've run away.
So pass along my many thanks to those fighter jocks on high,
Because of what they did today, we didn't have to die."

As I sit here wondering, what will the future bring?
Will the flight be peaceful, or will the Devil sing?
When will the fighting cease for good, so no more have to die?
All these things I ask myself, an hour before I fly.

— *Author Unknown*

The Spirit of Attack

Fighter pilots - John Labarre and Fred Tomlins - flew with me in Vietnam. The movies all show fighter pilots at a bar, so here are real fighter pilots at a real bar in a real war...

I wrote to my brother on Oct. 26, 1970: "One of my friends wrecked an F-100 last night. He landed short of the field, went through the base perimeter fence, bounced across a road and skipped thru a mine field! The plane was a total loss, but my friend walked away from it OK."

We had a saying: "Any night landing you walk away from is a good one!"

This F-100 carries CBU-42, grenade-size mines which we dropped on the Ho Chi Minh Trail. The CBU-42 is ejected downward. The air spins the mine, which starts the arming sequence. When it hits the ground it waits five minutes, then springs throw small clear fishing lines out, which hang in the bush. Anyone walking into the lines sets off the mine. There are hundreds of these mines on each fighter, and we spread thousands of them over the Trail. The mine carries a battery; when the battery dies, the mine is deactivated.

I'm getting better at holding the stick between my knees while taking the photo!

This F-100 carries four 500-lb bombs with "fuze extenders". These are three-foot pipes that go on the nose of the bomb so that the bomb is three feet above the ground when it explodes. This is very effective against troops in the open, especially in wet marshy areas where the troops can't dig bunkers. When the troops are in bunkers, we use delayed-action bombs which dig into the ground.
My Photo.

Page 70 **Bruce Gordon Stories**

Distinguished Flying Cross

The highest medal that I received during my flying career was the **Distinguished Flying Cross**, for a "Troops in Contact" mission. From a flying standpoint, it was a problem with weather in mountainous terrain which made bombing difficult. I knew that there were troops in contact, but I couldn't see anything but clouds, hills and trees. I was surprised to find that I had rescued an Army unit, and that their Commander recommended me for the DFC. Here is the citation which accompanies the award:

Major Bruce E. Gordon distinguished himself by extraordinary achievement while participating in aerial flight as an F-100 Tactical Fighter Pilot near Loi Tran, Republic of Vietnam on 16 January 1971. On that date, in support of an American company which had come under devastating attack, Major Gordon put on "the finest performance of close air support and precision bombing" ever witnessed by the ground commander. Braving a three thousand foot overcast, mountains shrouded in clouds, and ground fire, Major Gordon totally destroyed the hostile complex, saving the American company from certain destruction. The professional competence, aerial skill, and devotion to duty displayed by Major Gordon reflect great credit upon himself and the United States Air Force.

Saigon — 7th Air Force Headquarters

Six or seven months of flying combat missions was followed by duty at Headquarters in Saigon. This way, the people at Headquarters were all veterans who knew the flying mission well. I was assigned to the Fighter Plans office, and my job was to brief the Commanding General on our attack plans for the next day.

We worked twelve hours a day, seven days a week. At 7 AM the Intelligence officers would brief our office about what they found out in the past 24 hours. A team of 10 officers would allocate our available forces against these threats during the morning, including the weapons to be carried and timing of attacks. At 5 PM there was a big meeting—Intelligence would brief changes, the Army and Navy would brief their plans, and I would brief the fighter plans to the Commander. He would make changes and we would rush back to the office to send out revised messages. At about 7 PM we'd send out the last messages and adjourn to the Officers Club for supper and a beer. We slept in a guarded barracks in about a 12' x 10' room, and the cackle of the guards' radios made it hard to sleep. Each day was the same — but it was interesting to watch the development of the war. We were not allowed to bomb North Vietnam in a way to really destroy it. The political situation in the USA was getting worse, and we began withdrawing forces even though we knew the South Vietnamese were not strong enough to defend themselves. Soon I was working with the Army on final plans to withdraw.

Rabies (Hydrophobia)

Once or twice a month the pilots from Headquarters would go back to their original squadrons and fly a few missions to keep up their flying proficiency and to be aware of changes in the field. I flew from Saigon back to Phan Rang and flew with my Squadron. They had acquired two German Shepherd puppies which ran around the barracks and slept in one of the rooms. I finished flying several missions, and went back to Saigon.

I had been in Saigon for about a week when the phone rang. "When you visited here, did you play with the puppies?" "Yes". "Did you get your hands in their mouths?" "Yes—of course—you always get your hands in a puppy's mouth!" "One of them just died of RABIES!"

The news hit me like a blow to my stomach. "Tell me more", I demanded. "Everyone's getting the 14-day rabies shot treatment — one shot in the stomach every day for 14 days — guys are having bad side-effects and some are in the hospital, others suffer in the barracks". "Then the whole squadron must be GROUNDED!" I gasped. I was right — our whole fighter squadron had been grounded because pilots were sick with rabies shots!

The Spirit of Attack

The US Army built good roads in Vietnam so farmers could move their crops to market and the Army could move troops and vehicles. Paved roads made it harder to hide mines. Here is a typical small bridge with defenses. I think that good roads were a legacy of the war that Vientam will use for years to come.

*Typical Vietnamese village on the Mekong River delta.
I took these photos from an Army helicopter flying out of Saigon to a base camp.*

Now I was in trouble, and didn't even know it — all our phones were tapped by our own intelligence services, and I had just blurted out a SECRET — that a squadron was not ready to fight! About a day later I was called on the carpet to explain why I was so stupid as to reveal a secret over a telephone.

I had a more personal problem, though — would I die of rabies? I rushed over to the hospital and talked to the Flight Surgeon. He listened carefully to my story, and asked if I had any sores on my hands. *"Rabies usually causes a festering infection at the point of entry. You don't have any sores, so you probably didn't get infected. However, you can't be sure. I have the serum here to give you the 14 shots in the stomach, but they're bad shots and will probably give you pain, severe stomach cramps, and hives. However, if you don't get the shots and wait until symptoms of rabies appear, then you will die — there is no way to save you from a horrible death if you wait until symptoms appear. The choice is up to you.* **Do you want the shots?"**

What a decision — to endure 14 days of shots and agony, or to trust my luck, not take the shots, and risk a death caused by vomiting, choking, and insanity. A chill of fear came over me. I looked at my hands — no sores. **"Thanks for the advice, Doc. I won't take the shots. I'll go back to work and sweat it out".**

I went back to work, waiting the 15 days until rabies symptoms would appear. My throat was dry, and I imagined that death was creeping up on me. The critical days passed — and I was alive!

I later learned that this was the largest rabies crisis in the history of the US armed forces. The order was given that all pet dogs must be destroyed. There are sad tales of men crying as their pets are taken from their arms and shot. War leaves different scars on different people . . .

R&R in Hawaii

A combat tour in Vietnam was broken by one week of Rest and Recuperation, usually in Hong Kong, Australia, or Hawaii. The Saigon airfield was crowded with soldiers and weapons, weariness and war. I climbed the stairs to an airliner — and was met by beautiful stewardesses, air conditioning, and Hawaiian music playing softly! The psychological shock from war to peace was mind-boggling!

The long flight to Hawaii was nearly ruined by US Customs, who said I was violating copyright laws by carrying a number of pirated books, including Winston Churchill's "History of the English Speaking Peoples", etc. They detained me in Customs long enough so I missed my bus to meet Midge, who had flown out from Arizona to join me for R&R. I grabbed a ride in an Army truck with the baggage, and joined Midge for a week of love and relaxation before heading back to the war. When I got back on the plane to fly back to Vietnam, there was no music and the stewardesses were surly. The comedown was hard.

Last Flight

I flew 132 combat missions in Southeast Asia, then returned from Vietnam and moved into aircraft maintenance jobs. I loved aircraft and kept flying T-33's and the T-37 on test flights, but was getting closer to a desk job all the time. I didn't want to go to a desk job and resisted offers to go to the Pentagon or to Edwards AFB as a Maintenance Officer. I took a Quality Control job with the 4950th Test Wing at Wright-Patterson AFB, Ohio, where I could still fly test flights. Finally I took my last flight, in a T-37, in 1978. There was nothing special waiting for me. I parked the airplane at Wright-Patterson AFB in Ohio, filled out the forms, and walked to toward the hangar. I knew it was my last flight, so I turned around and looked at the planes for a last time. My flying career was over.

Conclusions

Q: How do you know if there is a fighter pilot at your party?
A: He'll tell you.

Q: What's the difference between God and fighter pilots?
A: God doesn't think he's a fighter pilot.

What makes a good fighter pilot? I talked to some Air Force medical personnel who were giving psychological interviews to prospective pilots. They thought that a good fighter pilot candidate would be a reckless person, most likely someone who loved motorcycles. Yes, we rode motorcycles for a while in Korea, but they were too dangerous for me. I felt confident that I was one of the best pilots in the US Air Force, but I wasn't reckless. I studied my aircraft books, I studied weather patterns, I learned about the propagation of radar waves in various weather conditions. I listened to my plane all the time; it was always telling me how it was feeling and how far I could push it. When it cried out in pain and flashed warning lights or rumbled or grumbled or surged, I immediately could guess what was wrong and do whatever it was needed. I took risks with a good understanding of what was involved—almost a cost/benefit analysis.

In World War II one of our aces said that fighter pilots are of two kinds: the hunters, and the hunted. The great majority of American fighter pilots are hunters, willing to tackle any odds. My mind goes back to the moment in Korea when our four F-106's raced to attack twenty MIGs and every man was in position, ready to do battle against terrible odds! "Live fast, die young, have a good-looking corpse!" was our graveyard humor. We'd been flying in Korea for a couple of months when a cartoon appeared on our wall with two vultures. One vulture says to the other: "Patience, my ass! I'm going to kill something!"

Attacking anti-aircraft guns is a very dangerous game, but I thought of it as big-game hunting. I've heard many stories of the "Wild Weasels" in Vietnam who deliberately flew their planes so the North Vietnamese would shoot missiles at them, so they could outmaneuver the missiles and attack the missile sites.

Fighter pilots stick together and keep the faith. When one of our pilots went down, we moved heaven and earth to get him back. I think of Bernie Fisher, who won the Congressional Medal of Honor in Vietnam by landing his A-1E fighter on a jungle runway in the middle of enemy troops to pick up a fellow pilot who had been shot down and could be seen hiding in the grass beside the runway. Bernie was willing to lay down his life for a friend. The Spirit of Attack is not limited to fighter pilots—I think of Army helicopter pilots who flew around with their windows open so they could hear the enemy shooting at them and could swing around to shoot back! Pilots from many nations have willingly thrown themselves at difficult odds, willing to expend themselves to protect their countries.

What makes a great fighter pilot? *Only the Spirit of Attack will bring success to any fighter aircraft, no matter how highly developed the aircraft may be!*

The Spirit of Attack

A defensive bunker on the perimeter of Phan Rang Air Base. A South Korean division defended us and terrorized the Viet Cong into fleeing the area. Close defense of the base was provided by our own Air Police. There were no real assaults on the base, just occasional hit-and-run rocket or mortar attacks.

"Last Flight". When pilots come back from their last mission in Vietnam, they are met by colored smoke, sirens, and a thorough dousing by a fire truck or two. The slight orange tint in the photo is from smoke signal grenades.

I don't have photos of my own "Last Flight" because I'd get wet and didn't have a camera. They hosed me down and had smoke flares just as in this scene.

My last flight was in a T-37. This one is at the Air Force Museum in Dayton, Ohio. All the planes that I flew can now be found in the museum. Maybe I belong in a museum, too.

Bruce Gordon Stories

The Spirit of Attack

Contributed Stories

Editor's Note: The following stories were contributed by my personal friends. Exciting things happened to me, and I knew they had also had exciting experiences. They contributed their stories to this book so that their experiences would be remembered in print.

Harry Shumate Stories

Harry Shumate's stories come first. He flew in the Korean War and I met him when he was flying F-106's in the 94th Fighter Interceptor Squadron in Alaska. After a brief statement of his origins, he describes several encounters with MiGs and getting a "probable" kill, then tells of being shot down himself. He mentions several names such as Gabreski and Kincheloe, great fighter pilot aces who are heroes to fighter pilots.

Philip Payne's stories are next. Philip tells of being part of an atomic bomb test, and experiencing the atomic blast from ten miles away. He upgraded from the F-86 to the F-102 and provides interesting technical data. I met him in Alaska with the 317th FIS flying F-102s.

Ray Janes was my Flight Commander when I got to the 94th FIS at Selfridge AFB flying F-106's, and together we intercepted a "Crate". Ray went to Vietnam before I did, and flew OV-10 Forward Air Control missions. He tells of the Vietnam War as seen from a FAC viewpoint, close to the action.

I belonged to the 94th Fighter Squadron which originated with Captain Eddie Rickenbacker in WW I. He was America's "Ace of Aces" in WW I. I had the honor of breakfast with Captain Eddie once, and I included one of Captain Eddie's WW I stories earlier in this book. During WW II the First Fighter Wing flew P-38s in North Africa and then in Italy and Sardinia. The First Fighter Wing flew F-106's in the 1960's and now in 2003 is flying F-15's in the wars with Iraq. I first saw "Mission to Remember" in Irv Styer's "1st Fighter Group Association News". It is one of the best combat stories I have ever read, especially as it has the story from both the attacking and defending sides. I edited the story extensively to put the comments from the Americans and the Romanians close to each other, and added comments to help follow the story. It is a fitting close for this book on the Spirit of Attack!

Korean War Combat

My flying career started at the age three when my Dad, who worked for a brief period as an aircraft engine mechanic, accompanied me in my first airplane ride. Over the years my interest grew, and in the third grade a very wise teacher allowed me to explain the operation of aircraft flight controls on the blackboard for the class. This was a highly motivating event in my young life. I worked in a furniture store during my high school years and spent most of my hard earned money on flying lesson at Bakers Field flying out of a 2,800' grass runway airport near my home in Port Huron, Michigan. Most of my ground school training for a private pilot license came through the Civil Air Patrol and reading every flying book I could get my hands on. All of my high school classes were selected towards aviation. I soloed two months before my 17th birthday in an Aeronca Super Chief. Later that year I was involved in a serious crash while riding in a J-3 Piper Cub with a pilot friend. My injuries included a broken back, arm, and nose, which kept me in the hospital for three weeks. I wore a back brace for several months and a large cast on my left arm for three weeks. Within six months though I was back flying again. In June 1945 I joined the Army Air Corps. Military pilot training had been cut off due to an overage of pilots at this time and the war was winding down. I finally got into the Air Force Aviation Cadet Pilot training program class 50-E in 1949 and graduated in September 1950 from Williams Air Force Base as a Jet Fighter Pilot. My first assignment was the 93rd Fighter Squadron at Albuquerque, NM flying the F-86A Sabre Jet.

In December 1951 I was a 2nd Lt in the USAF and left my two year old daughter and pregnant wife in Port Huron, Michigan for combat duty in Korea. We were on the Naval aircraft carrier "Cape Esperance" that had been converted into a transport for aircraft and personnel. There were about a dozen members of the 93rd Fighter Squadron from Kirtland AFB, Albuquerque, NM with me and about 50 new F-86E's. The MiGs had been having a heyday shooting down our B-29s and the US needed some high performance interceptor aircraft to provide top cover for the big slow bombers (B-29s) and older fighter-bombers (F-51, F-80,

The Spirit of Attack

F-82, F-84) as well as some Ausie and RAF aircraft. The Pentagon made clean sweep of every experienced U.S. F-86 pilot that had not already seen combat in Korea and had them on this carrier.

We were split up with half going to the 4th Fighter Wing at K-14 near Seoul under command of Col. Harrison Thyng and the other half assigned to the 51st Fighter Wing under command of Col. Gabby Gabreski at K-13 Souwon. I was assigned to the 51st Wing, 25th Fighter Squadron and B Flight. Ivan Kincheole, a Jet Ace, was my flight commander. We were transitioned into the new F-86E since we only had experience in the A model. The E had an advanced control system with a higher pressure hydraulic system and a full flying tail that allowed excellent control at the high mach speeds that were needed to combat the MiG. All the new guys were given a quick ground school and training flight to learn the new bird and then sent on a milk run combat flight to check out the combat area.

Probable MiG Kill

The events some nearly 49 years ago are far from crystal clear in my memory, but these are the ones that stick in my mind. I was on my 55th mission flying number four in the flight. We were flying a large left oval sweep just South of the Yalu river at 38,000 feet near the Supung Reservoir. On the first northeast leg of this pattern I spotted a couple of MiGs far below us heading north going home. I called them out but flight lead Col. Gabby did not see them. In a few seconds they were out of my view and no action was taken. The next circle and in about the same location I spotted a lone MiG going the same direction as the first one. I immediately called in. Gabby looked for about two seconds then said "Four go get him! Three, you cover." At this time the MiG was below me about 15,000 feet. I rolled my Sabre over on its back and pulled hard on the stick to set up on the MiG. I was vertical with speed increasing fast into supersonic range and then the unforgivable happened, I lost sight of the MiG. In my frustration I rolled my plane and reduced power. As I completed my vertical roll I again spotted the MiG straight below me and our distance was closing fast. I opened the speed brakes and at the last moment he flew out from under me. I pulled hard back on the stick while going full power and putting in the speed brakes. A full miracle occurred on this pullout, as I arrived within 300 feet of the MiG with speeds synchronized, and on the tail of the MiG dancing in his jet wash. I could hardly believe what was happening. There was the MiG in my sights with a high tail, wing fences, and a mid-wing. I squeezed the trigger and the six 50 caliber machine guns fired into that Commie MiG. He lit up like a Christmas tree as the tracer bullets found their target. The first burst raked across the top of the fuselage of the MiG and into the cockpit. He immediately pulled up into their typical evasive climb maneuver. I fired several more bursts with each one hitting the MiG. Fuel was streaming from the MiG and I was concerned about him blowing up and flaming me out since I was so close. His jet fuel was obscuring my wind shield but I could see him smoking from the engine area and streaming fuel from both wings. It was then Joe Moen, my wingman, called out that other MiGs were coming in on us. With some reluctance I broke off from the attack and we evaded the MiGs. During the debriefing I later talked to Joe about the mission and he said he never saw the MiG until we pulled out on its tail. The vertical dive with the roll, then the speed brakes going out and in, was a very unusual maneuver to say the least but it got the job done. He did say that it was the most beautiful bounce he had ever seen. I never received a kill for that mission, only a probable since he was only smoking and not on fire or didn't eject. I fired over 1500 rounds of the 1800 we carried at that MiG and saw hits every time. If he made it back and landed I seriously doubt if that plane ever flew again.

Close Call

I was flying on the wing of Ivan Kincheloe; we were a flight of two having split off from the rest of the flight. We spotted a flight of four MiGs heading south at 40,000 feet about half way from Pyongyang and the Yalu. They had spotted us and started a shallow left turn back north. We were on the inside of their turn, cutting them off, and hoping to get into gun range. As we were closing to about 2000 feet, I saw six MiGs back at 7 o'clock doing the same thing on us. I called them out and since they were out of range, Kinch said to keep them in sight. We kept playing this game with us closing on the flight of four MiGs and the flight of six MiGs closing on us.

Harry Shumate tells his crewchief of his MiG kill

Harry Shumate Stories

I was getting a little uncomfortable and as they continued to get closer. Kinch said "you call it and I'll be with you ." Finally, when I could see the air divider in the intakes of the MiGs I called "break left." As we snapped our wings down in the turn, the MiGs opened up with their cannons and the golf ball size tracers came streaming by. It is surprising how hard you can pull on the stick and how many G's you can tolerate when you are being shot at. Two of the six MiGs tried to stay with us as we went into our hard diving turn, but we slung them out. The other MiGs climbed up and then a pair of them dove on us as soon as we lost the first two. They were playing a yoyo on us with six against two. We kept breaking with diving turns and the golf balls were flying by every time we let up. We were running out of altitude, fuel and energy. The fatigue from all the G's and the combat was getting to us. I was trying to stay on Kinch's wing while trying to evade the cannon fire. Finally, out of desperation, I pulled the controls as hard as I could and when south came up on the horizon, I rolled wings level. In this desperation maneuver I lost the MiGs as well as Kinch. I learned later that he did the same thing. We were still in radio contact and both in the clear, so we joined up on the way back home to K-13. I was totally amazed during our intelligence debriefing that Kinch gave a detailed account of every maneuver we and the MiGs made. He went on to give the precise description of the markings on these aircraft and that they were the new MiG-17, an advanced version of the MiG. This was the first that they had been seen in this theater of operation. It was no surprise when Kinch returned to the states that he was selected for test pilot school and went on to set many speed and altitude records flying experimental aircraft at Edwards Air Force Test Center. I was glad to get through this mission with out any holes in my aircraft or me and did not observe the details he did.

The MiG-15 "Fagot" could fly higher than the F-86, but was unstable in a high-speed dive and was a poor gun platform. Its one 37mm and two 23mm guns were bigger than the six .50 caliber (12.8mm) F-86's guns. Those bigger MiG guns had a low muzzle velocity which forced the MiGs to shoot farther ahead (lead the target more), a disadvantatge in a tight turning fight.

Barracks happening between flights

The scene was the spring of 1952 at K-13 Air Force Base Suwon Korea. We were members of the 25th Fighter Interceptor Squadron flying the F-86E Sabre Jet. The weather was lousy so we were not getting much action and time was dragging. During these slow times young healthy fighter pilots start looking for things to do. We were in tin huts that masqueraded as a BOQ (Bachelor Officers Quarters) listening to music over AFN (Armed Forces Network radio transmitting out of Tokyo Japan) when a great idea developed. We decided to play a trick on our Flight Commander Capt. Ivan Kincheloe. We were all 1/Lts and some of these so-called tricks were not thought through for the possible consequences. Our fearless leader Kinch was bending his elbow at the hut up the road that was our Officers Club so this was a excellent opportunity to work our devilish trick. Willy Guinther had a combination radio-tape player-recorder and had recorded some of the better music from AFN. Curt Eskew who a great speaking voice played the part of an announcer. We dubbed in a news broadcast into one of these music segments that went something like this " We interrupt this program to bring you news from Panmunjom—United Nations Representatives have settled with the North Koreans on a peace initiative—now we will return you to studio one for more good music." Panmunjom was the meeting place that straddled the 38th parallel where the top people from both sides were trying to work out an end to the Korean war. Joe Cannon was stationed at the door to alert Willy of Kinch's approach. As he came bounding in with all of the latest news from the club Willy was over in the corner and started the tape running. THEN Kinch heard that news broadcast! WOW what a reaction. He ran out the door and yelled Wizz has to hear this! Wizz was Major William T. Whisner an ace fighter pilot and our Squadron Commander. We were all bent over laughing at how well we did with this joke on Kinch. Then we realized that the top brass in our outfit might not appreciate the humor of our joke. We ran down to Wizz's hut but his bunk mates said he was already gone and on his way to Gabby's hut. Gabby was Col. Francis S. Gabreski Commander of the 51st Fighter Wing and the leading Fighter ace of the Air Force. With ever increasing fear we ran to Gabby's hut , but a worse scenario was developing. He was on his way to headquarters' to call FEAF command post in Japan. FEAF was Far Eastern Air Force that commanded all air activity in that part of the world and was just one step below the Pentagon. I'm not sure what really happened during that call to Japan. The Col. was breathing fire when he returned and we got our buts reamed out very smartly and were lucky not to receive a court martial.

Ground Attack

In March of 1952 I was a member of the 25th Fighter Interceptor Squadron Flying F-86E North American Sabre Jets from K-13 Suwon AFB Korea. Our primary mission was to engage and destroy enemy aircraft attempting to bomb or strafe our ground forces or shoot down any United Nations aircraft. On this mission we were a flight of 4 that launched about one hour ahead of the group of about 40 F-86 aircraft. Our task was to check the weather and report any enemy aircraft in North Korea that might pose a threat to our forces. We were interested in the east half of north Korea from the 38th parallel to the Yalu river.

The mission briefing was short and sweet since there were only four birds and no wheels around in the wee hours of the morning. My aircraft crew chief had everything ready to go. Our maintenance personnel were very conscientious and thorough with our aircraft. If their bird shot down a MiG they took credit for it, the pilot was just riding along!!! They took great pride in painting Red Stars on the side of their aircraft for every MiG kill. We cranked-up and checked in. Our flight call sign was Robin. I was Robin 4 therefore the last one to check in. The 25th used birds for their call signs. Our takeoff was at the first light before sunrise. We climbed out in loose formation and after passing Panmunjon and DMZ (demilitarized zone) at the 38th parallel, we armed and check-fired our guns. The E model had six 50-caliber machine guns. You can hear them very clearly since they're mounted beside the cockpit and fire out the nose of the plane. The smell of cordite is strong as the gun smoke is sucked in the intake. Some of the F models that came in after I left were configured with four 20-millimeter cannons. The 20s had a slower rate of fire but took a much bigger bite with an explosive warhead. We checked in with control and we were advised that they had no traffic for us at that time. We followed the east coast keeping it off our left wing tip. The sky was clear with no contrails. It was just about 200 miles from K-13 to the mouth of the Yalu River. That took us a little less than 30 minutes and gave us 30 to 40 minutes to hunt MiGs before Bingo fuel. Bingo was set at 1,500 pounds for the F-86 which gave us enough gas to get home make an approach and one or two go arounds. Many times we pushed the limits due to being in the middle of a good fight having MiGs all over you and using extra fuel diving and making high G turns to stay alive. Once two of us had to land at K-14 Kimpo AFB, about 20 miles north of our base. I was reading zero on my fuel gage and Willie Guinther the other pilot flamed out on the taxiway.

We turned right at the Yalu and flew northeast parallel with the river. As we approached the Suoungho reservoir we spotted a long train on the south side of the river in a deep gorge going for the rail bridge just down river below the big electric power dam on the Yalu that formed the reservoir. This was a premium target. It was undoubtedly a re-supply train carrying material and personnel for the enemy. If we could knock out that locomotive and stop that train the fighter-bomber guy in F-84's and F-80's could destroy the boxcars and their contents. We flew over the sizeable lake and pickled off our drop tanks. We would occasionally call drop your "Cadillacs" since a pair of tanks cost about as much as a new Caddy. Lead called "brakes out." We extended our speed brakes and followed in trial formation in a near vertical descent until leveling, "brakes in" and we were at about 200 feet above the surface of the lake. Our speed was Mach .95 (just under supersonic) and I was experiencing some wing roll that occurs near the speed of sound in the Sabre. We hopped over the dam then dropped down to the river to the level of the bridge. The formation was spread out so that we had about 1/4 mile separation so we could aim independently at the train as it was crossing the bridge. The enemy knew the dam was a high priority target so both shorelines were lined with cannons, machine guns, rockets and small arms. They must have heard us fly over before we let down, because they were sure waiting for us. Since I was number four they had a little extra time to aim at me. I was dancing in the jet wash of the three 86's ahead of me as I tried line up my sights on the locomotive. It had already crossed too far to the right for me to fire at the engine, but I did get the tender and the first car and chipped lots of paint off the bridge. The time that I was in range of the various weapons firing at me was a few seconds, but it seemed much longer to me. It was a shower of tracer moving from both sides crossing all around me. It is difficult to see how at least one shell did not hit my plane. In looking back at the geography of this area, the gunners must have been firing level or even down a little at me, with the result of shooting at each other. There must have been several killed on both sides of the river.

Harry Shumate taxies out at K-13, Suwon Airfield

The Spirit of Attack

  I quickly joined my flight as we climbed out. As we turned south our track took us over a good size town and they opened up with well place anti-aircraft fire. I remember from World War II hearing about ack-ack being so thick you could walk on it. Well there was a large square, black with exploding shells off our left wing at exactly the same elevation. We instinctively turn to the right and climbed. Within five seconds there was another burst straight below us and higher than the first. We made a hard turn back to the left and increased our angle of climb. There was one more big burst under us but much further away. We were out of their range now and could start breathing again. I was so very glad our primary mission was intercept and not ground attack.

Harry Shumate's F-86E in Korea

Shot Down

  On May 13th 1952 I had my last and most harrowing mission in my Korean combat tour. We normally flew 100 missions to complete our combat tour and this was my 93rd. As you near the end of your time in combat you are either glad to see it coming to an end or as in my case, disappointed that I did not have many chances to lead flights and shoot down MiGs. I was going to make the best of the remaining missions that I had to fly and maybe knock down a couple of MiGs. The F-86 Sabre Jets had run up an excellent combat record against the MiGs with a real kill ratio of 12 MiGs destroyed for every F-86. We credit the pilot training, esprit de corps and tactics for as much of the final results as the superior engineering of the Sabre. On this mission I was an element lead, number three in the flight. A young new, rather inexperienced, Second Lieutenant fresh out of flight school and combat crew training was flying number four on my wing. This was a routine fighter sweep just south of the Yalu river in north central Korea, flying a big racetrack east and west looking for MiGs that would try to sneak through and get to our fighter-bombers and ground forces.

  We had only been in this area a short time when we were alerted by combat control (our ground radar) that MiGs were coming into this area. I spotted a flight of four MiGs heading north slightly below us at about 15,000 feet. I was cleared by our flight lead to engage them, so I immediately set up behind the lead MiG. The MiGs apparently spotted us because they started a shallow left climbing turn, their typical evasive maneuver when being bounced by our aircraft. My young wingman was way off to my left and slightly ahead of me, not a good tactical formation. Lead and number two were far to our right and slightly below us. Hawk leader called "Hawk four break left " so my young wingman made a hard left turn. I looked and did not see any aircraft behind number four, so I thought I could get one shot at the MiG in front of me. I no sooner turned my head when both lead and number two were screaming "Hawk 4 break left". I then looked over my left shoulder and there were 8 to 10 MiGs in rather close formation at about 300 feet and closing in on me. The lead MiG was belching fire from all three of his nose cannons. I immediately started a full control hard left turn when it felt like I'd been hit by a truck and the whole plane shook. My left rudder pedal went limp and was swinging freely. I continued my roll until I was on my back, then pulled the nose towards vertically down. Looking back, the only thing I could see was a lot of white smoke, but no MiGs were following me. I announced over my radio that I was hit. I guess the MiGs saw me trailing all that smoke and thought I was going straight into the ground so they broke off the attack. Within a couple of seconds after going vertical, I noticed the yellow low hydraulic pressure warning light blinking on my instrument panel. I then attempted to pull my plane out of the dive. The controls were frozen rigid, with no response. I instinctively fed in some nose up trim while pulling on the stick and flipped the speed brake switch open, but nothing happened. There I was, going like a bullet straight down and no controls. I pulled back the throttle and was getting ready to eject, then my prayers were answered; the hydraulic pressure built back up temporarily and the trim I had fed in pulled the plane to level flight. The plane had no sooner leveled off when the controls locked back up again. I went from 38,000 to 23,000 feet during this out-of-control dive.

The Spirit of Attack

Bailout and Rescue

During this whole ordeal the rest of my flight were chasing off the MiGs that shot me up. Combat Control meanwhile had stopped the whole air war and was vectoring in aircraft to my rescue. Soon I had many flights of other F-86s' offering me protection. I learned later that the alert aircraft at both K-13 and K-14 were scrambled to help out. In one of the aircraft that joined me was Jim McCauley of the 16th fighter Squadron. He said he would stay with me and escort me out of the area. My controls kept going in and out as the hydraulic pressure went up and down. It would sometimes cause the plane to jerk into a roll or pitch up or down. It was an interesting ride. I found that I could control the plane better if I slowed to a low cruise speed. Jim pulled up close to check my battle damage and reported a large hole about 6 feet behind the cockpit right over the engine and another hole in the right wing flap where it attaches to the fuselage. In spite of this damage the plane was running very smooth except for an occasional jerking on the controls. I knew there would be no way I could land this bird. It was about 100 miles from where I was hit to the Chodo Island where the rescue aircraft orbited off the North Korean mainland. My energy now was directed on keeping this bird right-side-up until I could rendezvous with the rescue guys. I rehearsed the ejection procedure in my mind and pulled all my parachute straps snug. At about 50 miles from Chodo, I started a slow descent from 21,000 to 6,000 feet. The flight controls remained locked most of the time. I could get one or two small movements, then they would lock up again. The jerks were less frequent but thoughts of landing were out of the question. A few weeks before another F-86 had a similar problem and he had a very hard landing and severely damaged the aircraft and broke his back which caused him to be paralyzed from the waist down. Jim McCauley was doing an outstanding job staying with me and giving words of encouragement. I checked my fuel and noted that I was slightly below Bingo which meant there was not enough to safely get home. I asked Jim about his fuel state and he said " don't worry about it, I'm staying with you ". He was committing himself to running out of fuel just to help me. The radar controllers were doing a good job of giving me directions to intercept the rescue aircraft which was a SA-16 Grumman Albatross amphibian with the call sign of "Dumbo". As I got closer to the SA-16, I really looked intently for him because I did not want to attempt to do a 360 with my control situation. I spotted Dumbo at one o'clock about 8 miles away. He was going straight towards me at about 2,000 feet altitude. I was straight and level at 6,000 feet indicating 250 knots. As Dumbo disappeared under my nose I started my ejection procedure, first leaning slightly forward, I pulled up the right arm rest that fired the canopy straight back and off the aircraft, next I pulled up on the left armrest which locked my shoulder harness. I then sat up in the seat in preparation for the ejection and squeezed the now exposed trigger on the left armrest that fired the ejection seat. Note: The state of the technical advancements in ejection seats were very crude at this time. The ejection machinery was a long tube attached to the back of the seat likened to a cannon barrel with a 20MM cannon shell in it and the pilot in the seat was the bullet. When that seat fired it is hard to describe the shock and force that hit me. The best way I can describe the sensation is that it felt like a giant hit the bottom of the seat with a sledge hammer as big as a house. The next second I was in the 250 knot wind blast, that was very much like a tornado, with my arm flailing around and tumbling head over heals. This kick in the butt and wind blast erased all the pre—planning I had done. All I could think of was to open the parachute, so I immediately pulled the ripcord. Instead of opening the chute, there was the ripcord dangling in my hand. I realized, in my panic, I had neglected to open the seat belt to free myself from the seat so consequently the parachute would not open. But I was as I was falling and tumbling I thought that MiG didn't kill me but now I'm going to die because of an unopened chute. I wasn't about to give up so I proceeded to try to claw the chute open. As I reached back to get at the chute I felt the seat that I was firmly strapped to. *"Oh you dummy"* I thought and then opened my lap belt. I immediately separated from the seat and as the wind caught into my chute I felt that wonderful tug as the chute deployed. Looking up at that big orange and white canopy was the most beautiful sight I could imagine.

I looked down from I'll guess 2,000 feet to the water and there was Dumbo landing. Then Jim came flying by, and as I waved to him he rocked his wings. My next thought now was not drowning

SA-16 Grumman Albatross at the USAF Museum, Dayton, Ohio

Harry Shumate Stories

in the Yellow Sea but I had another problem. I had done too good of a job tightening my harness; if I popped the Mae West life vest, it would crush my chest. I then struggled with the harness to loosen it, but the tension from the parachute risers would not let me open the buckle to the strap across my chest. The water was getting closer. I remembered the Japanese knife in my flight jacket, so I pulled it out and proceeded to cut that strap in two. I pulled the lanyards on both sides of the Mae West and it filled out fully. It would have broken my ribs and cut my breathing off I'm sure if I had not been able to cut that chest strap before inflating the vest. I had one more look at Jim using his valuable fuel circling above just before hitting the water. I plunged into the water and stripped off my parachute harness and bobbed up to the surface. The water felt cold as you might expect at the 38th parallel, but my adrenaline was pumped up so much that I didn't really notice it. There were large swells bobbing me up and down but I could see the amphibian taxiing on the water about 300 feet away and my Hero Jim flying over rocking his wings again. Then Dumbo finally taxied over to me, and proceeded to turn around and back up to me. In our rescue briefing and training we were told that this backup procedure might be used so I was not alarmed. The large swells could have put me up into the rotating props of that flying boat as it taxied near me. A big husky crewman on the Dumbo reached out and hauled me aboard. I stripped out of my wet flight suit and climbed into a size 50 pair of long johns underwear. They then strapped me on a bunk and bounced and bounced in the high swells for a long time before becoming airborne.

I was checked into the hospital back at our base and had to have six stitches in my chin. I guess the chest strap hit me on the ejection ride. My back was also very tender from that giant kick in the butt. I left the next day for an R&R to Japan that I had previously applied for—talk about good timing. I phoned home from Japan and learned my wife had given birth to a baby boy and the child had some serious medical problems. She had already contacted the Red Cross to request my return home. My 93 missions were considered enough to complete a combat tour and I was placed on status as an Operational Evadee since I was shot down in enemy waters. This status got me home faster than an emergency leave and also gave me a priority on the selection of bases. I was assigned to the 172nd Fighter Interceptor Squadron at Selfridge AFB Michigan, which was about 45 miles from my home. My son died 2 months after I arrived home of Addison's Disease.

To borrow a phrase from Paul Harvey " and now the rest of the story". Jim McCauley, my faithful escort stayed with me all the way. I later learned that the rescue plane lost sight of me in the high waves after it landed. Jim however was in continual radio contact with them and circled around so as to fly over the Dumbo and went straight towards were I was bobbing in the water. They made a slight turn and in about one minute had sight of me. The Navigator on the Dumbo was in an open hatch of the nose taking pictures with a home movie camera. Only when the Dumbo could confirm positive sight on me, did Jim leave for home. He was way below Bingo fuel so he climbed towards home until he ran out of fuel and flamed out. He climbed to about 25,000 ft. He was close enough to glide back for a perfect landing at K-13, coasting to the end of the runway and tapping his right brake and turning off on the taxiway. The plane was inspected, fueled, run up, and flew on the late mission that day. This was outstanding airmanship by a real hero.

The MiG-19 "Farmer" had two engines in a fatter fuselage, and max speed of Mach 1.2 Early models had stability problems.

Phil Payne Stories

Atomic Bomb Test

by Philip E. Payne

My squadron commander called me in one day. I suppose every 2nd Lt. has some trepidation when called into his commander's office. Reporting with a sharp salute he asked if I would like to go on a cross-country flight with him to Salt Lake City. Since I was only a 2nd Lt. and very eager to build-up my flying time, I quickly said, "Yes Sir." He then told me that we would also be stopping at Nellis AFB, NV for a special event. We were to participate in an Atomic Bomb test!

Needless to say this announcement caused a few tingling feelings to shoot through my spine. Everyone knew that Atomic Weapons testing was being conducted in the desert north of Las Vegas, NV, but we knew very few of the details. L/C Spencer also knew very little about the tests, except that our part was to be a low risk, information gathering and orientation mission.

Visions of being tasked to fly through the fireball of a blast came to mind. Worse, I could just see us becoming sterile from the radiation. Such was the little grasp we had on the effects of an atomic weapon detonation. We were not directed to bring along any special flight gear, nor were we provided a list of required personal equipment. This lack of information just heightened our anticipation of what we may encounter.

My Squadron Commander, Robert V. Spencer, and I packed a flight bag on a Thursday afternoon and departed Whiteman AFB about 3pm. A flight bag consisted of a flexible hang-up clothes bag, which would fit over the radios in the nose compartment of a T-33A. After a fuel stop at Kirkland AFB, Albuquerque, NM, we arrived at Nellis AFB just as it was getting dark. The lights from the Strip glowed brightly as we landed in Las Vegas. After checking in to our VOQ rooms we hitched a ride to the Down Town area of Vegas, and had dinner. Food is one of the real bargains in Las Vegas. Back at Nellis AFB we turned in early, not really knowing what the test would require us to do.

The next morning we arrived at the designated building on Nellis AFB for briefing and mission planning. The fact that we were selected to participate in an atomic bomb detonation gave us reason to speculate on the part we would play in the up-coming test. Soon, however, our speculation of a wide range of possible events was kaboshed. We were told that we would be positioned some ten miles from ground zero (Ground zero is the actual site of the detonation). In sum we were to fly the T-33A at a specific point relative to the bomb burst, which was to be held on Jackass Flats North of Las Vegas. Jackass Flats has since become very popular in the news media because many underground detonations have been carried out in that area. Our involvement was to be a flying one and our position was to be North of the shot (an atom bomb test is called a shot).

During the mission briefing we were told to be at 20,000 feet above sea level, on an easterly heading, about 10 miles north of ground zero. The exact position was displayed on a large wall-map. We were given individual maps with our route and timing annotated on each map. Further, we were to arrive on station in advance and fly our assigned route a few times. This was to assure that we would be at the correct position at the precise assigned time. Ground Zero for this shot was to be 1,500 feet above the floor of the desert; the weapon was in a balloon, tethered from a tower. The desert floor was very flat for several miles around ground zero. While flying this mission, we were to follow the directions of a central air control authority, which would provide directions to assure that we were correctly positioned at the time of the shot. During the preflight briefing, we were told that we were not to fly through the mushroom cloud. Nor were we to make any comments over the radio about what we observed before, during or after the shot.

The briefing also included a presentation of what we could expect to experience at the moment the bomb was detonated, and afterwards. They described the very bright light that would occur at detonation and the safe guards we needed to take. We were told to NOT be looking toward the blast at the moment of detonation; a countdown to detonation would be transmitted over the UHF Guard channel. They then issued us an eye patch, and told us to wear this patch over one eye at detonation. Even with the patch over one eye, we were to look away from ground zero, or down into the cockpit floor. We were also informed that we would definitely be close enough to feel the shock wave generated from the test shot. And, that the jet would shake and roll or pitch slightly as the shock wave from the blast passed us.

At the time we were surprised how little the briefer told us. When we would ask questions, we received very simplistic answers. L/C Spencer pushed for more information but we were politely told, "You do not have a need to know that information." This statement, as we discovered later when we began to carry missiles with nuclear warheads, was a guiding principle of all operations involving atomic weapons. Nevertheless we were somewhat excited about the mission. They did inform us that there would be other aircraft flying in support of this test, but that on our planned route we would be well clear of other participants.

They also instructed us that once we were released from the test (test was over), we were to return directly to Nellis AFB. Upon landing, we were to follow a specially marked truck to a specific parking place, and stay in the cockpit, with the canopy closed and the jet engine running. Ground crews would be there to go over our plane with Geiger counters to check for any radiation contamination.

We were also told that it was not likely that our T-33A would acquire any radiation. However, if our jet did have any measurable radiation level, we would be directed to taxi to a different location, where our plane would be washed-down with high-pressure soap and water, and decontaminated. After we were advised that all was safe, we would then be directed to taxi to the Base Operations parking ramp. Then when the plane had been rechecked for contamination, we could shut down our engine and exit our jet. Upon exiting our jet we were to stay next to our T-33A while each of us would personally be checked, to make sure we were not hot. Hot, meaning we would have become slightly radioactive from the nuclear particles emitted from the atom bomb shot.

Finally it was time for the mission. We took-off on time, contacted our air space control agency, and were directed to our orbit area. We had about thirty minutes to establish the correct orbit. By flying our rectangular orbit, timed such that we would have a line-of-sight to the bomb ground zero point just aft of the right wing we developed our orbit timing. The actual device was attached to a gondola of a balloon that was about 1,000 feet above ground level. L/C Spencer was a stickler for using a checklist, especially for new and different events. After the briefing he had drawn up a checklist of things we needed to do during the mission. We reviewed every item on his checklist at least twice. We even practiced putting on our eye patch.

The black heavy cloth patch that we were given blocked practically all light to one eye. Having been cautioned NOT to look at ground zero at the time of the blast or we could suffer permanent eye damage, we wanted to be safe. L/C Spencer and I discussed exactly what we would do and where we would be looking at the time of the blast. He decided that he would wear the patch over one eye, shut the other eye, and bury his head in his lap. I decided to wear the patch over my left eye, since it was not my dominant eye, and look down into the cockpit floor with my right eye open. As soon as we had seen the bright light from the detonation start to decrease, we would then turn and look at ground zero.

We were in orbit almost an hour before the shot, a continuous countdown was transmitted over the emergency radio frequency. So we always knew just how long it was until the test. We wanted to assure that at least one of us would have good vision for landing. I had seen several training films on atom bomb shots and thought I was prepared for the bright light that accompanies a shot. Not so clear was the possibility of radiation contamination, or danger of the shock wave that accompanies a shot. Radiation you can't see so you need to have some type of special detector to measure possible contamination. The most common device is the Geiger counter.

The Geiger counter actually counts the amount of neutrons emitted from the decay of radioactive material (usually a form of uranium). Being in the presence of an atomic event, if you are close, can result in you and or your clothes becoming radioactive. You or your clothes can actually emit gamma rays and beta particles. When you are contaminated you are said to be 'Hot'. Gamma rays are like very strong x-rays. Perhaps you have observed a laboratory technician in a doctor's office. X-rays are fairly low-level compared to atomic radiation. Even so, X-ray technicians are serious about being behind a lead barrier, and they always wear a lead-lined apron.

Radiation sickness is serious business. If you have even a slight dose of radiation you can get very sick, but you usually recover. A higher dosage and you lose your body hair; your body becomes susceptible to almost any disease, and receiving big dose you die in a matter of hours. I suppose these and other related thoughts were going through our minds as we waited for the shot.

Most of the information we were allowed to see and study indicated that the chance of harmful radiation exposure from an atomic explosion was slight for two primary reasons. 1) Most damage, both directly from such an explosion and from flying debris, occurs very near the explosion fireball, or directly down wind from it, and 2) The intense heat that exists near ground zero is so high that one is quickly vaporized or simply cremated.

Finally, the time was near to time zero, and we were right on the prescribed orbit and location. I was flying the plane, and as I said, I had put the patch over my left eye and was to be looking down, with my head down, into the cockpit. As the time was counted down to zero, I can remember that I was holding my breath as I heard 5, 4, 3, 2, and 1! Then, everything went white, I mean it was so bright you could not see the floor of the plane. Then a very odd thing happened, I could actually see through the floor of the cockpit and see the ground below us! Yes, I could see the ground THROUGH the floor of the plane. I also could see a bright light even in the eye over which I had the patch. I find it hard to describe the brightness of the bomb blast. It was not like anything I had ever seen. It was, very much like how I had envisioned that the brightness one would experience if in the presence of God.

Later when being debriefed by the Atomic Energy team members that ran the Geiger counter over us, I was informed that they had had similar events told by other crew-members that had flown in atom bomb shots.

In only a few seconds after the blast the air controller said, "You're cleared to look at the mushroom cloud." We removed our eye patch and looked over our right wing. It was something to see. A fast rising billowing cloud of dust was still flowing out and up. The fireball was quickly subsiding and winked out as we watched. As you have all seen on TV or in the movies, the cloud when fully developed, looks like a big elongated, very tall mushroom. Coming out in a circle around ground zero I could see a very fast traveling shock wave. We were breathless, and couldn't seem to talk for several seconds. Then we both began to talk excitedly about what we had seen, THEN!

We could see the shock wave coming; it looked just like a supersonic shock wave. Although there were no clouds to show us the shock wave, you could see the light being bent, like looking down into the surface of a lake and seeing the waves caused by wind. The shock waves warped our view of the desert below as it rapidly approached us. We both grabbed hold of the controls and again held our breath. When the shock wave hit us it was like a big hand had grabbed us and moved us about 300 feet away from ground zero. I have seen similar shock waves since, one was when an F-111A was traveling supersonic just above the ground, and the shock wave was causing dust to be raised over the desert floor.

After that we became spectators and watched as an F-89D fighter flew back and forth through the mushroom cloud gathering samples. Bet his plane was radioactive hot when he landed! But, we were told to return to Nellis AFB and land, so we did.

As briefed, a crew met us with a Geiger counters. With our engine running they went all over the plane and gave us an all-clear signal, so I shutdown the engine. As soon as we exited our jet they began to go over us personally with Geiger Counters. No significant level of radiation was found. After the debriefing and answering lots of questions they cleared us to leave for our home base. The strange thing about the debriefing was the apparent lack of interest in the fact that I could see through the floor of the plane when the bomb detonated. The debriefers listen politely, stated that they had had similar reports from other crewmembers that had flown on similar test, but were not very interested in pursuing it further. This event, of course, left a big question in my mind. I always think about Superman's X-ray vision, and wonder what it would be like to be able to see through brick walls when you wanted to. But, I have never had another similar event in my life. This sight phenomenon was something I will never forget.

Supersonic Flight

My flight logbook says that by 1963 I had more than 1,000 hours in the F-102A. At that time period this was one of the most modern fighters around. It was the second fighter that could achieve supersonic speed in level flight.

Flying supersonic is a strange term because it isn't just one speed. In flying terms it is referred to as Mach 1. What it really is, is the speed at which sound travels through the air. Although a function of the temperature of the air, it is about 1,100 feet per second at 250 centigrade at sea level. Speed of sound varies with temperature and at altitude can only be detected by instrumentation, but there can be visual signs. The warmer the temperature of the air the faster sound travels. At low altitudes during a moist day (high humidity) as you approach the sound barrier (Mach 1) the air will condense around the leading edge of the wings and canopy of the airplane. This condensation appears as white streamers, somewhat like contrails, but you have no trouble seeing through it. There are a variety of changes that are associated with flying supersonic.

One significant aerodynamic change is a change in the center of lift. As you go supersonic the center of lift on the airplane wing shifts toward the rear, and a nose-heavy condition is experienced. This nose-heavy condition is not severe and after a few times transiting the supersonic speed, you hardly notice it as you automatically re-trim the aircraft flight controls. As you go subsonic again, the center of lift shifts forward, causing a nose-light condition and the aircraft may "dig in" if you're applying back stick as you go subsonic. Another thing that happens is a large jump in the flight instruments.

As you can imagine the air speed and altimeter do not transition from sub-sonic to super-sonic in a smooth fashion. As you approach super-sonic speed the altimeter and air speed appear to hang-up, or stop increasing or decreasing. Then as you are past Mach 1 the air speed indicator jumps to your new speed, and the altimeter rapidly goes round and round as the pressure levels near the sensors change. It was exciting to watch the gages fluctuate as you crossed the sound barrier; going faster than the speed of sound in the F-102A.

F-102 Missile Firing

The F-102A also had incorporated some large changes in the traditional way fighters were built. Because it was primarily an interceptor for bomber aircraft, it was equipped with missiles rather than guns. This turned out to be a poor design decision that was not rectified until the Viet Nam war. The F-106A, the early models of the F-4, the F-86D and other fighter interceptors of that generation were built without a gun. But, more on Viet Nam later.

The F-102A carried 6 missiles; a normal load included three radar guided missiles and three heat-seeking missiles. New Air Force commanders believed that the days of "dog fights" had passed, that speeds were too fast to have a turning fighter against fighter battle. Boy, were they wrong. The air-to-air, unguided rockets did get put into the F-102A, but they were mounted in tandem; one behind the other, in the doors that covered the missile bay.

The missile bay occupied most of the underside of the fuselage; from just behind the cockpit, back to the landing gear area. Each missile was mounted on a launch rail on a trapeze mechanism. When the missiles were to be launched, a complex sequence of doors and launcher movement was required. As the F-102A fire-control system anticipated the missile fire signal, four large doors underneath the airplane opened, exposing the missile bay. Then the three front missile launcher trapezes were extended, to place the missiles below the aircraft. A rail launch arrangement could then be used. Once the missile bay doors opened, and the launchers extended, the three front missiles were ripple fired at intervals of about 300 mili-seconds. When the front missiles had been launched and a "missile gone" signal was received by the fire control

Convair F-102A "Delta Dagger"
USAF Museum Photo Archives

system, the front three launchers were retracted. Then the aft three launchers were extended and their missiles fired. When all missile launchers were safely retracted the missile bay doors closed. Of course, if all six missiles were to be fired, when the front three launchers started their retract cycle, the rear three launchers started down, and the rear three missiles were launched as soon as the front launcher rails were retracted. This sequence occurred every rapidly, and six missiles could be launched in just a few seconds. Perhaps the thing that amazed me most was the fact that the four folding missile bay doors and six launchers were operated by compressed air.

That is right, I said, "Air pressure." Three large fiberglass, spherical shaped bottles held 3,000 pounds per square inch (PSI) air pressure. Before each mission a special ground-servicing unit pumped these storage bottles to 3,000 PSI. I remember one day, one of these bottles broke loose at its bottom air pressure connection while it was being serviced, and BOOM! Like a rocket it shot-out right through the top of the aircraft, just behind the cockpit. It looked very much like an anti-aircraft cannon shell had hit it from below. The metal of the plane was bent up like a can when a big firecracker is set-off inside it. One unusual event remains in my memory about the F-102A radar.

Because of the poor long-range detection of jet aircraft by ground based radar, interceptor pilots were constantly trying to find their target at long range. Because of the need for a fighter to make a successful intercept with minimum direction, pilots were continuing to strive to detect and track target aircraft as far out as possible. The long-range mode of the radar and the pilots display scope in the F-102A was limited to 40 miles in the normal search mode. In the search mode the normal 3-degree radar beam was wobbled to cover more area, and provide tracking capability. When pilots were a long way from their target aircraft (greater than 100 miles) and had nothing else to do, we started experimenting with the F-102A ground-map radar mode that had a range of 200 miles. In this mode a non-spinning, 3-degree beam was used. Soon we developed ways to detect a bomber at 120 to 130 miles out using this ground map mode.

When we described this capability to the radar manufacturer (Hughes Aircraft Company) they laughed and said, "That is not possible. If you examine radar range calculations you will see that there is not sufficient energy reflected from an aircraft to allow detection beyond 40 miles."

We finally got one of the local 32nd Air Division Staff pilots to try our technique, and he quickly became a believer. He called the Hughes Factory and talked to their chief test pilot. Reluctantly he agreed to come to our base and see what was happening. He did, and following our techniques he too detected a B-47 at 140 miles and tracked it all the way down to missile launch range. Then he said, "This is interesting, but it may just be a fluke, not every plane will work like that." But, he flew three different planes and had similar success in every one of them. Being convinced, he called the radar experts at Hughes and told them they better get out their slide-rules (an early day logarithmic computer for engineers). This discovery was a great boon to our morale, and we received a very prestigious award for developing this capability that wasn't even known to exist.

Early in the days we began to fly the F-102A we were sent to Tyndall AFB, Panama City, FL to fire gunnery (rockets and missiles). Their weapons range was completely over the Gulf of Mexico and they had both towed and free-flight targets for live firing.

The first time we went to Tyndall AFB we only fired air-to-air rockets. Rockets were carried in the forward part of the four missile-bay doors. Six rockets were mounted in each door; three rockets in tandem; a total of 24 rockets. When a full load of rockets were fired, the front three rockets were fired first, with each departing front rocket completing the firing circuit for the other three rear rockets. The first time we fired rockets I think every pilot was surprised at the noise and jar associated with the movement of the missile bay doors.

Cleaning the mess from firing a full load of rockets from the F-102A was a chore. Rocket blast was directed up and into the missile bay covering everything with black soot. Soon we only fired six rockets for training missions, to minimize the mess. Missiles were slow in coming to the 326th FIS. Realize that this was a completely new jet, with a new weapons system and everything did not become available at one time. Like any new fighter, we also were experiencing the 'groundings' as safety items were added and systems modified. Weapons and weapons systems were often modified to correct design flaws and increase capabilities.

The Spirit of Attack

Rockets were not new and were pretty simple for the F-102A. Soon we were eager to move on to missiles. I will never forget the first missile I fired. I wanted to do as well firing the missile as I had shooting rockets the first time. I was required to make three dry runs against a B-57 towing a rag banner with tin foil in it for radar reflectivity. Because we were firing missiles the banner was now 15,000 feet (about three miles) behind the tow aircraft. Similar to rocketry we had to separate the radar returns of the tow aircraft and the banner, and then lock-on to the banner before a "clear to fire" radio call was given.

Everything went as planned and at the fire signal I could feel the missile launchers come down and SWWWOOOSH! Away the missile went. I looked up to see if I would hit the banner. But, the missile did two or three corkscrew motions and then headed straight down at the Gulf of Mexico. Everyone said I was shooting at fish, HA! In those early days of missiles, that happened many times. Because there weren't many missiles available and each cost a bunch, I did not get to launch another one on that trip to the range. The next time we went to the range I did get one to guide but I didn't hit the banner; it did get very close and was declared a kill.

*F-102 flies past erupting Augustine Mountain.
This volcano is an island in Cook Inlet southwest of
Anchorage.
Photo by Bruce Gordon, 1964*

*It's hard to take photos from a single-seat fighter while you're flying in formation with another plane. You have to set the throttle, put the stick between your knees, grab the camera and take a photo before you are too close or too far from the lead plane. You are moving at several hundred miles per hour, so we would get past this volcano in a couple of minutes. Your fuel is always low, so you can seldom come back for another photo.
A photo like this is a once-in-a-lifetime event!*

Ray Janes Stories

A 94th FIS ORI

In the Air Defense Command there was a system of inspections called the Operational Readiness Inspection which each unit had to endure each year. This inspection was in addition to all the others but this one was the killer that determined the reputation of the unit. Usually we learned it was imminent through the grapevine that existed between units so we knew vaguely when the ORI team was to visit and could be somewhat prepared. They looked at everything in the unit but the exercise was the most important part of the inspection. If we weren't able to generate a certain number of sorties and be credited with a certain number of kills the unit failed and the team could be expected to return shortly to give the unit a final chance to pass before heads rolled. Amazingly enough they always walked in with a smile on their face and said, "We're here to help you." Their real mission was to nitpick the unit on the slightest thing.

One of the last ones I participated in before I was sent to Vietnam was in 1967. I had just taken over as a Flight Commander and was still leaning the capabilities of the pilots and they were taking their measure of me. When the ORI team showed up I called my flight together. When we were sent home to await the start of the flying phase of the exercise I told them, "Each of you has flown many exercises and this one is no different. All you have to do is the job you've been trained to do and we'll come out fine." Little did I know what was in store for us on this one.

Surprisingly the flying started in the early afternoon instead of at night. We were called using the telephone tree and reported as soon as possible. We were briefed and assigned out aircraft and set them up for a scramble. Our targets were the usual T-33s at altitude and for spice some B-57s with Electronic Jamming equipment would also be used.

The scrambles began and the T-33s were hit with satisfactory reliability and the aircraft were returned to base to gage the ability to turn them around for a second wave. We believed this was when we would find the low altitude targets and the jamming B-57s. My flight was the first one off and committed against the low altitude targets. To our surprise the controller broke radio silence. We usually used Data Link transmission into our flight computer for directions to the target, but he said he couldn't direct us to the targets because electronic jamming was too strong and blanking one of the radars where the targets were flying. I had experienced this problem in Alaska against some B-52s so I asked him to direct us to the center of the jamming signal and keep us there until we could find the target visually.

He gave us a vector to the target and we flew to the area at medium altitude since the target could be above or below us. Once he told us we were in the area I directed my wingman to search high while I searched low

The trick to find an aircraft visually is to "keep your head on a swivel" and look for movement in the air rather than the aircraft itself. My wingman had no luck but I spotted some movement at low level and directed him to stay at altitude to act as a radio relay and to spot any other traffic in the area. I dropped to the rear of the target and below his altitude to enable my radar to look up at him and not be clouded with a return signal from the ground. I was surprised to find the B-57 flying at 1500 ft. altitude because that was the minimum we were allowed to conduct low intercepts. Legally, I wasn't supposed to fly below him and find him on the radar by looking up. So I leveled behind him and locked on to him using my Infrared sensor, which didn't detect ground clutter but also didn't give the range to the target. I kept him in visual sight until I was close to the range to fire and switched to radar and "burned through the electronic jamming" to see the target on my radar and locked onto him. Then I speeded up to complete the intercept and get the fire signal. I climbed back up to altitude and briefed my wingman how to get a fire signal on the radar. He did and I sent him home while I stayed in the area to direct the rest of the fighters onto the target. This was known as a trailing aircraft, which would track the target visually while the other fighters joined the trailing aircraft and were directed onto the target. When I got low on fuel I briefed the flight lead on the procedures and had him take over and guide the rest of the flight onto the target. We scored 100% kills on the target while the other flights couldn't find the target and when they did couldn't get a fire signal.

The Squadron passed the ORI and was commended for its success because other squadrons hadn't been able to handle the situation. I was lucky in that I remembered the early manual, which explained the use of trailing aircraft to direct F-86s onto jamming targets, which blocked out the ground radar, and I had been exposed to the tactic in Alaska. This is why experience counted so much in the Air Defense mission since the pilot was charged with overcoming any obstacle to kill the target since a target missed might mean a city destroyed. Besides the last tactic was ramming the target and nobody wanted to trust the manuals explanation on how to do it "safely"!

A Shaky Flight

Selfridge Air Force Base held its 50th anniversary in 1967. The base was built in 1917 and became know as "The Home of the Generals". During the 50th anniversary there were many dignitaries including about 32 Generals formerly assigned to the base. The guest of honor though was Captain Eddie Rickenbacker known as America's Ace of Aces from World War I.

He was happy to come and participate in the ceremonies as he had done in the past. One of the things we always did when he visited was to tow the SPAD aircraft out for display. The aircraft belonged to the Air Force Museum and we had restored it to flying condition though we were forbidden to fly it. After Captain Eddie had graciously posed for pictures much the same way he had in France during WW I our Wing Commander, Col. Converse P. Kelley announced that he was going to fly the SPAD.

We were all surprised of course but also pleased. He donned his leather helmet and goggles and mounted up. He called *"contact"* and the Crew Chief spun the propeller to get the engine started. After a short period of shaking and spewing smoke the engine settled down and the Col. gave the signal to pull the chocks. Pictures were snapping all over the place and movie cameras were whirring. Everybody was grinning from ear to ear.

He taxied to a clear spot on the grass and ran the engine up and began to bounce over the ground. Finally the tail came up and the plane lifted off the ground as the wings dipped back and forth. He climbed up to about 1,000 ft. and flew around the field a couple of times. The wings continued to rock back and forth. He turned on final and came down to the ground and immediately ballooned back into the air. He floated for a while and finally touched down again and his bounces weren't enough to get him airborne again. He taxied slowly back to the parking area and shut off the throttle. He waved to the crowd and a great cheer went up and people clapped their hands. He climbed out of the plane and seemed to have a little trouble with his knees. But he walked over to Captain Eddie and grasped his hand. Those of us who knew him noticed he was white as a sheet. He gasped Captain Eddie's hand and shook it with both of his and I overheard him say, "I don't know how you guys did it"! Captain Eddie just smiled. Later one of the Generals said to Col. Kelley. "I guess you know your career is over don't you." "Of course, he answered, I planed it this way." He retired the next summer and the Air Force Museum took back our SPAD informing us the flight was illegal and trucked it back to the museum. The last time I was there it was on display with the note that the personnel of Selfridge Air Force Base restored it but failed to note that it was probably the last real SPAD ever flown and that Col. Kelley was the last pilot to fly one. I think he went out in style.

A Small Error

Not long after the F-102 was armed with the nuclear GAR-11 missile elaborate procedures were introduced to try to make certain a nuclear war wasn't started by accident. The primary system was called the "Two Man System". That meant that two people had to agree to the final decision to employ the weapon. That is a little hard to do in an aircraft with a single cockpit. The solution was to use a code system called Authentication Procedures. Each pilot, dispatcher in the alert hangar and Ground Controlled Interceptor (GCI) controller had the same codes that had to match before the weapon could be employed.

Sounds simple but it really wasn't. The idea was if a nuclear equipped aircraft were to be scrambled the authentication code would have to be used by the GCI controller and the dispatcher before the aircraft would be cleared for take off by the tower. Then the pilot would have to use the same type of authentication procedures with the GCI controller before employing the weapon.

Soon after the weapons were loaded on five-minute alert aircraft I was scrambled from Eielson AFB in Alaska. We went to the aircraft after the scramble horn sounded and started up. When we called for clearance to taxi we were given clearance to take off by the tower. We roared out of the hangar and made a rolling take off as soon as we turned onto the runway. We assumed that the authentication procedures had been followed and lit the afterburners. Just as I rotated the nose to lift off the tower called "Abort, Abort, Abort". It was too late for me to do that so I continued the take off while my number two aircraft was able to abort. As soon as I was airborne and had the gear up I called the tower and asked what happened. They told me a mistake had been made and I was to land as soon as possible. That presented me with a slight problem as I was armed with a nuclear weapon and very heavy with fuel. I told them I would have to burn some fuel out to land safely and would get down as soon as I could.

I put out the speed brakes and lit the after burner and pulled it to the minimum and began a climb to about 20,000 ft. The tower continued to call me with orders to land "Now!" and I continued to say as soon as I burnt some fuel. When the drop tanks were nearly empty after about 15 minutes of flight I called for landing instructions and was cleared to land. I was still very heavy so I made a high G approach and landed at the maximum safe speed for the tires and the drag chute. I held the nose in the air as long as I could and braked as much as I felt safe and used all 12,000 ft. of the runway. I taxied back to the alert hangar and got on the phone to the GCI site to find out what went wrong. It was very simple. We had been pulling alert with the nukes on 15 minute to allow time for the authentication procedures to be used. That week the powers that be decided that the nukes should be prepared to go to war and changed them to 5 minute alert. Both the GCI controller and the dispatcher "forgot" the nukes were on 5 and didn't authenticate.

About the time I rotated the battle commander at Elmendorf realized the wrong call signs were taking off and called the abort. As we talked we all agreed that it was an embarrassing situation and since no harm was done we would all just forget about it. When my heart slowed down I realized that I might have been the first pilot to fly an F-102 with a nuke aboard. Then the crew chief came upstairs to the quarters and asked me how I did it. When I asked him what he meant he said, "Well sir, you landed the aircraft very heavy and the brakes are still good and I don't see how." I laughed and told him it was just superior technique that came from long experience. He went out shaking his head. He thought sure he was faced with a brake job for the aircraft and I doubt if they stocked them there. That would have surely let the cat out of the bag and caused an investigation.

It's A Crate!

Bruce Gordon and I were on five minute alert at Galena AFS Alaska one winter day when the scramble horn sounded. We rushed to our aircraft while the dispatcher authenticated the order to scramble birds armed with conventional missiles and a GAR-11 nuclear missile. We knew it was serious when we were scrambled because the birds armed with conventional missiles would normally have been scrambled.

After take off we were given a vector toward the Bering Sea. The controller told us that they had something on their radar but they had no idea what it was. It would appear and disappear from time to time and it appeared to be a slow mover. The controller wasn't sure but what it wasn't some kind of weather phenomenon. We flew out as a flight and when we arrived in the area of the blip we couldn't see a thing. We separated and searched high and low. It was one of those golden winter days with the sun low in the sky and the light from it seem to make the ice covered sea a flash of gold while the sky was a piercing winter blue.

Bruce spotted some movement at a low level and we dove down to investigate. When we got down to low altitude we lost radio contact with the GCI site. We could hear the controller

Captain Eddie Rickenbacker points to the 94th Fighter Squadron emblem on the Spad at Selfridge AFB in 1967.

talking to us but he could not hear our transmissions. As we neared the target it appeared to be a C-47 painted white but with red stars on the wings indicating it belonged to the Soviet Union. As we flew past we couldn't see through the window and the aircraft immediately took evasive action as we went by at about 1500 ft. while it was flying at about 500 ft. Bruce circled over the aircraft while I climbed to 15,000 ft. to reestablish radio contact.

The controller was amazed when I reported what looked like a Russian C-47. He checked with our headquarters and learned it was a Russian version of the C-47 called the Crate. They wanted pictures of the aircraft so Bruce attempted to snap it. He dove to 500 ft. and slowed to minimum speed with the landing gear down and the speed brakes out. As he passed the Crate he was attempting to fly the F-102 at minimum speed, focus the camera and snap a picture. He was controlling the aircraft by holding the stick with his knees and using the rudder. Just as he moved past the Crate and took the picture the Crate turned toward him. Obviously trying to cause him to fly into the Bering Sea. It was a very jagged surface with large chunks of ice sticking up from the surface. No doubt if Bruce followed the natural training for formation flying he would have dropped down and may have caught a wingtip on the ice and crashed.

"Captain Eddie" Rickenbacker congratulates Colonel Kelly on flying the Spad in 1967. Capt Frank Cheshire of the 94th Squadron holds the helmet. It was probably the last time that a WW I Spad has been flown. That Spad is now in the Air Force Museum with different markings.

As I saw what was happening I immediately considered the turn a hostile act and armed my conventional missiles. If Bruce did hit the ice and crash the Crate was going down too because I was so angry at their attempt to cause him to crash that they were never going home either

I had no time to report what happened because Bruce showed superior flying skill by pulling up his gear and closing the speed brakes as he lit full afterburner and staggered up above the turning Crate. I thought the blast from his afterburner might cause the Crate to crash and would have been happy to see it happen but it bounced around a little bit and turned back toward Russia less than 50 miles away.

Since Bruce was safe I disarmed the missiles and reported what had happened to the controller. He said that headquarters would like more pictures but I told him we might violate Russian airspace if we tried since the Crate was flying toward its home. He agreed and gave us a vector back to base and said the Russians were scrambling their MIGs so it was probably a good idea to go home and avoid an incident.

We returned to Galena and landed safely. During the debriefing with the controller we learned that headquarters was unhappy that Bruce only got one picture. I told him we would have to have been crazy to try again with the MIGs up and the next time there might have been a mid air collision which would have really caused an incident. Headquarters scrambled an F-102 from Elmendorf AFB to pick up the film and later we heard it was confirmed as a Crate. They never really determined why the aircraft was flying so close and so low but the general consensus of opinion was they wanted to determine how soon our radar would pick up a low level target. That must have been it because that is the only time they tried to penetrate our airspace with a low level Crate. Or maybe their pilots weren't crazy either.

Vietnam Stories

My first assignment in Vietnam was to the 1/9th Air Cavalry Squadron. It consisted of three troops with one troop assigned to each Brigade. I lived at Phouc Vinh with the FACs at first and then with the 1/9th Field Grade Officers. The Headquarters of the Squadron was stationed at Phouc Vinh, C Troop, Squadron Maintenance and the headquarters of Company H 75th Rangers

The Spirit of Attack

better known as the LRRPS which stood for Long Range Reconnaissance Patrols. They were six man patrols inserted into the jungle to keep track of enemy movements, ambush patrols to acquire documents for intelligence purposes and sometimes even capture prisoners for interrogation. They might set an ambush, kidnap a prisoner, gather documents or just watch and report. They were out for a few days or up to a week. Often they had to be extracted under fire after they were discovered. They were usually dropped off several klicks from their target position and walked into it and set up a perimeter. They tried to sneak in and out but often that wasn't possible. They were armed with claymore mines, hand grenades and small arms. We periodically checked on them by radio and they always whispered or just clicked the mike if they had nothing to report or the enemy was nearby and they didn't want to talk. Often when they were discovered they had to withdraw while fighting and sometimes they had to run a long way to the LZ for pickup. They had to be in superb shape and fearless.

Volunteers would report to the Company Headquarters and be put through a rugged training program. The most visible part of their training was running around the base in the hottest part of the day carrying a pack filled with rocks. As part of their training I was asked to brief them on the need for USAF air strikes if they were in serious trouble. Most of the time they were able to return from their mission without any trouble or with organic 1/9th or Division firepower. I had ridden on UH-1 Lift ships on team insertions and extractions. I had seen them in their camouflage uniforms with their faces painted to match, loaded with ammunition and weapons and rations they would need for the several day mission. I also saw how tired and worn they were when they were extracted. So I was surprised one day to receive a radio call from the Squadron Tactical Operations Center asking me to contact the Troop Commander in the Area of Operations where I was doing my VR to help extract a LRRP team.

I had been flying a Visual Reconnaissance mission and really didn't expect to have any action because I had been briefed before take off that I probably couldn't get any air strikes for any target I found because all the strikes were allotted to a big action in some other part of Vietnam. I was scheduled to put in a preplanned strike on a target identified by the Division some time before. The Army jealously guarded these strikes because they were allotted so many per day for their targets. However the targets were often several days to two or three weeks old. Most of the time FACs referred to them as Monkey Killer Missions or Turning Trees into Toothpicks because we were rarely able to report any meaningful Bomb Damage Assessment. But the strikes were an agreement between the Air Force and the Army and the Army was very upset if they didn't get their allotted share of the strikes.

When I contacted the Troop Commander he told me the team had been inserted the night before and they had been surrounded by at least a company of enemy soldiers. They were receiving heavy fire and had several wounded. They needed help immediately. I asked him why artillery wasn't hitting the area and he said all the tubes were committed to other missions. Then I asked about inserting the Blue Platoon or the Quick Reaction Company on standby.

He told me the enemy force was considered too large for either the Blues or the Quick Reaction Company. Then I asked about attack helicopters and was told there were none available. All this sounded very strange to me because I knew the Army had a lot of assets and none was available in a desperate situation like this. Then it dawned on me. The Army had written the team off because they would probably kill them with friendly fire if they committed any of their assets and they had already had enough incidents of killing their own troops so let the Air Force take the blame. That made me angry and I decided I was going to get them out if I had to do it with a bluff of possible air strikes by firing my White Phosphorous marking rockets.

When I contacted the team it was immediately obvious to me how desperate their situation was. The radio operator was screaming, instead of whispering to conceal their position, because the enemy knew where they were and there was no need to try to keep it secret. I knew the radio operator was very near to losing his ability to think straight so I asked him in a very calm voice to tell me the situation. He said

Soviet IL-14 "Crate" similar to the one that Ray Janes and I intercepted off the coast of Alaska. This one is at an aviation museum in Russia.

The Spirit of Attack

they were receiving fire from all sides and several team members were already wounded and perhaps dead. He expected to be over run at any moment. I asked him to pop a smoke so I could determine his position and he said he couldn't because of the heavy fire. I asked him to tell me some terrain features and after I thought I knew where he was I fired a marking rocket and he estimated his position from the white smoke and said that the enemy fire lessened for a short time but was now heavy again. His voice was rising again and I knew I had to calm him down. I told him I was going to get them out but when I started they must keep as low as they possibly could because I was going to have to put the bombs so close that a lot of shrapnel would be going over them. He said he was already flat as a pancake and couldn't get any lower and still fire his weapon. He added that they were almost out of bullets anyway. They had fired their claymore mines and couldn't throw grenades because the fire was too intense.

I called the Division Tactical Operations center to make sure there was no organic firepower available and was assured that all the artillery and attack helicopters were engaged. I knew that probably wasn't true because I didn't hear much radio traffic showing battles in progress. I requested an air strike and was told there was nothing available and then I asked to use the preplanned strike and it was denied. I was given permission to contact the Direct Air Support Center (DASC) my luck there as a last chance to redirect the preplanned strike. When I contacted the DASC I was told the same thing. I said I had troops dying in the field and there must be something available. I was told there was nothing available for at least an hour and probably longer because all the alert birds were being refueled and rearmed. I then asked them to divert the preplanned strike and it was denied. I asked to speak to the supervisor and he came on the radio. Fortunately I recognized his voice as a FAC I knew. I asked him if his initials were BF and he said yes. I explained the life and death situation and asked again to divert the strike. He said he couldn't do it without getting into serious trouble. I told him to blame me and I was prepared to take all the heat and if he wouldn't do it I would make a stink by starting charges to publicize the situation.

I was sure neither the Army nor the Air Force wanted that to happen. Then he agreed to divert the preplanned strike that was due in minutes.

I went back to the LRRPs team channel and told the radio operator the strike was on the way and to reconfirm their position. His voice was calm now and I was shocked when he gave me the coordinates. He was calling the strike on his own position. I asked him if he knew what he was doing and he answered in a resigned voice, "It doesn't make any difference anyway. We're all dead anyway." I told him that wasn't true and reiterated that I was going to get them out and he said in the same voice, "OK". I told him again to hug the ground as I heard the flight check in. They had eight 500 lb bombs and 20 MM guns so I think they were F-100s but I'm not sure. I briefed them on the situation and told them I wanted the best bombs they ever dropped. I intended to mark for each bomb and the first pass for the lead aircraft was to be from west to east and number two would attack from east to west. I knew that was hard for them to do so that was the reason I was marking each bomb. There were no questions so we went to work.

I put the first mark about 50 meters south of the team's position and told lead to put his bomb just to the south of my mark. He did and as he came off the target I rolled in and put a mark about 100 meters north of the smoke from the first bomb. When he was off the target I put a mark about 50 meters west of the target and told him to attack from south to north and put his bomb 50 meters west my mark. He did and then I put the next mark east of the target and told number two to drop from south to north and put his bomb just east of my mark. After that was done we had boxed the team's position and I put the next four bombs just outside that box. The radio operator came on the FM screaming that I had done it and they were running. I told the fighters to use half of their 20 MM to box the smoke that the enemy was running and that should send them on their way but I wanted them to hold the second half of their ammo to make sure the rescue birds got in safely. They did another magnificent job so I told the Troop Commander to get the Lift birds in there as soon as possible and he told me they were already inbound.

They picked up the team but I never knew how things turned out because one was KIA, four were WIA and the radio operator was babbling and repeating all the transmissions he had made during the action. They were all evacuated to Japan so I never got a chance to talk to them. After the lift birds made the pick up without any fire I told the F-100s to hose the area just in case any of the enemy were still running or still alive in the area. They did and I congratulated them on excellent bombing and gave them 50 KBA as an estimate. I couldn't get in to check for sure because the Army attack helicopters were busy continuing the chase. The Lift ships reported numerous dead enemy bodies in the area but had no real number because they were busy helping the team onto the helicopters. I wrote a letter to the squadron commending the pilots and another to the DASC commending the support but never heard a word from either the Air Force or the Army about the action. I considered it one of my best days as a FAC because I got all but one of them out alive though I thought we would be lifting bodies instead of soldiers.

The Day I Blew Up A Mountain

Day flying over the Ho Chi Minh Trail in Steel Tiger for me consisted mostly of flying specialized missions or VR (Visual Reconnaissance). When I was flying VR I had to have a really good target to get an air strike but often I would get fighters that had been diverted and had to drop quickly. So during my VR I would track areas that seemed promising and when ABCCC (Airborne Command and Control Center) would offer to give me those quick strikes I would pick an area nearby where I suspected something was going on and expend them. Sometimes I got good results and sometimes not.

One day I was flying the last mission of the day, which meant I would be touching down just as the sun disappeared. It was early in the mission so I first went to an area I had been observing for several days that was the furthest out. I planned to work my way back to the most active part of the trail in case the NVA (North Vietnamese Army) decided to get an early start that night.

The area was thick jungle but there were numerous places where it looked to me that there were a lot of active trails that seemed to come together at the base of a Karst mountain. Soon after I flew over the area I got a call from the ABCCC with the offer of a flight of fighters if I had a good target. I told them I had an area that looked active and I sure would like to probe it with a strike to see if there was something good there. They said the fighters were very low on fuel and could only make about two passes. I told them to send them to me. The fighters, F-4s with Mark 82s, came up on my frequency almost immediately. They were a little far out so I had plenty of time to get into position, brief them on the target and be ready to fire a Willie Pete marking rocket as soon as they had me in sight.

I briefed them to make their passes along the side of the mountain and to put their bombs as close to the base of the mountain as they could get them. I told them I hadn't seen any ground fire but that it was an area with a lot of active trails. I rolled in and fired the WP and told them to try and put their bombs between my mark and the mountain. The first F-4 put his bombs just where I wanted them and I told the wingman to hit long and I would follow him in for another mark. He did a good job and I rolled in to follow his path.

As I rolled out to fire the mark I could see under the trees because of their hits and the area under the trees was filled with newly built hooches, OOPs, I mean military structures. They were the golden color of new structures rather than the gray of older buildings. I fired a rocket into a hooch and cleared them hot to walk their bombs from my smoke further along the side of the mountain. They told me this was their last pass and they had to drop everything they had. I followed them in again and could see numerous burning hooches, secondary fires and explosions and caves in the side of the mountain. There were many more hooches under the trees. I was sure we were either into a big base camp or storage area. I thought it was a base camp because I didn't see any trucks for hauling material. I complemented them on their work and credited them with a BDA (Bomb Damage Assessment) of about 20 military structures plus some secondary fires and explosions.

When I called ABCCC I told them we were into something big and I would take all the fighters I could get because it looked like a wide area of lucrative targets. They sent me two more flights of F-4s and said that was all I could get because everybody else was dumping their loads and going home because of the approaching darkness. I didn't argue but I thought we had at least two more hours of enough light to keep probing the target. I was just happy that I could get some strikes on a good target for a change.

The next flight checked in and had a little more fuel so I was able to walk the bombs around uncovering more hooches, starting more fires and setting off more secondary explosions. The flight departed happy with their BDA. The third flight checked in and I briefed them that we seemed to have pretty much destroyed the hooches I could see and I hoped they could hit some of the caves.

They didn't seem too happy about that but agreed to try. It meant they had to fly toward the mountain and drop far enough away to hit the cave and break clear without hitting the Karst. It certainly wasn't an easy assignment. I put in the mark and told them to hit any cave they could see around my smoke. They rolled in and started dropping one bomb at a time. They were all over the place. They hit up the side of the mountain and the open ground in front of the caves several times so nothing happened. Finally they said they had to unload and go home. I put in another mark and told them to try to hit the cave next to my smoke. Lead rolled in and I watched the bombs disappear into the cave. The last fighter was right behind him and his bombs disappeared also. There was a short period when nothing happened so I told them they hit it perfectly but I couldn't give them any BDA. Just as I said that the whole mountain shook violently and seconds later smoke and dust started floating out of the cracks in the top of the Karst.

I said I couldn't tell them what was going on but the whole mountain was periodically shaking violently and smoke and dust was coming through the cracks on the top. I said it seemed to me that they had set off numerous explosions inside the Karst. They didn't sound too happy with such a nebulous report and went home. I continued

An OV-10 Bronco over the Ho Chi Minh Trail during the Vietnam War. It has a 230-gallon droppable fuel tank and 2.75" White Phosphorous rockets for marking targets.

to watch the mountain for some time and it would sit there quietly and then suddenly shake violently and more smoke and dust would belch out the top of the mountain. Obviously bad things were happening inside the mountain. I watched it happen time after time. Finally I decided to look over the rest of my area and check it again later.

I covered my VR area and didn't spot anything that I thought I could get air strikes for so I flew back to the mountain about two hours later. I was amazed to find it was still periodically shaking with smoke and dust spewing out through the cracks in the top of the Karst. I reported my sighting to the ABCCC and told them it was still a good target in my estimation. They replied that everything was being held for the night missions so I called it a day and returned to NKP. It turned out to be the right thing to do because the sun set as I taxied into my parking space. I had only made a couple of real night landings in my tour and I was out of practice.

The intelligence debriefing didn't go very well in my estimation. The Lieutenant that debriefed me seemed to have only one answer for every thing I told him. "We'll check further but that is an area of no known enemy activity." The fact that the bombing was excellent, probably the best results I ever got using F-4s, and that what appeared to be a whole village of at least fifty large hooches destroyed didn't appear to be of much interest to him. The description of the best F-4 bombs I ever saw dropped setting off explosions that were still cooking off after two hours was of doubtful usefulness to the war effort.

He did offer to keep checking to see if any of it could be verified. By this time I was used to debriefer's indifference to anything outside their area of interest and really didn't care about much of anything anymore so I just said I would look forward to hearing any information that could be gathered about the mission. By the time they got around to fragging an RF-4 to check, the trees and brush would have grown back and all they would see was some empty bomb craters because everything else would have been cleared away. I had learned in SVN that since it was such a bad luck place the enemy would probably never use it again.

I went back to my BOQ room, gulped down a martini, cleaned up and went to the club for dinner. I never heard another word about the mission. If I ever decide to visit Vietnam again I would like to try to check their records on that date and see if there is anything about losing a mountain. But I imagine their intelligence officers were as reluctant to report losing a mountain as ours were to confirming it.

The Spirit of Attack

OV-10 Bronco assigned to the 1st Brigade, 1st Air Cavalry Division at Tay Ninh City, South Vietnam. Note the heavy load of external fuel tanks that it carried, in addition to a pod of 2.75" white phosphorous (WP) rockets for marking the target. These aircraft were used as Forward Air Controllers (FACs) and spent many hours flying over the Ho Chi Minh Trail. When they saw a target, they would call for fighters, then mark the target with WP to show the fighters where to drop their bombs. Photo from Ray Janes.

Ray Janes in Vietnam in 1969 with his OV-10 Bronco while assigned to the 1/9th Air Cavalry Squadron at Phouc Vinh. Left to right: Sgt. Davis (Maintenance NCOIC), Maj. Ray Janes (Pilot), John Paczkowski (Crew Chief). Ray Janes Photo

WW II: Mission to Remember

The 1st & 82nd Fighter Groups over Ploesti

The oil refineries in Ploesti, Romania provided Nazi Germany with essential fuel for its armed forces. Several raids by B-24 Liberator bombers made the Germans aware that the oil refineries provided the life blood of their war effort, and they greatly increased air defenses. A low-level attack by B-24 bombers on August 1st, 1943 was a disaster and led to the use of P-38 fighters.

The B-24's flew from North Africa across the Mediterranean Sea to the Balkan mountains. By flying at low-level, they hoped to come in under the German radar and achieve surprise. Radio silence was mandatory. The mission went badly from the beginning. An aircraft in the lead flight had serious engine problems and had to ditch in the Mediterranean Sea. The lead bomber turned around and went back to watch his friend ditch in the water. The lead navigator and mission commander were no longer in front, and the lead was taken by a backup navigator who was less-well prepared. The raid was to follow a railroad into Ploesti, but the navigator picked the first railroad that he saw and turned along the wrong railroad. Other aircraft saw it was the wrong railroad and broke radio silence, calling "Wrong Turn! Wrong Turn"! Half the bombers followed their leader down the first railroad, while the others continued straight and turned down the originally-planned railroad.

The Germans heard the "Wrong Turn" radio calls and alerted their air defenses. They had a special railroad train with many antiaircraft guns which went down the railroad track in the same direction as our bombers. Our bombers, following the railroad at low level, were brought under heavy antiaircraft fire from a train traveling directly beneath them! The first group of bombers on the wrong railroad discovered their mistake and turned toward Ploesti. The changed route meant that the two groups of bombers arrived at Ploesti at low level traveling in opposite directions at almost the same time. Delayed-action bombs dropped from one group were exploding as the other group passed over at low-level. Antiaircraft fire, exploding bombs and smoke screens and aircraft coming from different directions confused everyone. As the bombers headed home in broken formations, masses of German and Romanian fighters decimated the bombers. 54 of the 117 bombers in the raid were lost.

Headquarters decided that the B-24 bombers had failed and that this extremely important target should be attacked by our long-range P-38 fighters carrying bombs. This turned into one of the most exciting battle stories of WW II.. I now turn to the story written by the men who were there, including a view from a Romanian pilot. I have edited to piece it into a single story of a huge air battle.

Credits: John Mullins, whose excellent book "An Escort of P-38's" is the source of my quotes from Herb "Stub" Hatch, whose first-person story is quoted extensively. Dan Vizanty, Commander of the Romanian fighter squadrons that attacked the P-38's. Irvine Styer, editor of the Fall 1987 issue of the First Fighter Group Association NEWS.

The Spirit of Attack

The 1st Fighter Group, consisting of the 27th, 71st, and 94th Fighter Squadrons, fought in North Africa and in Sardinia before moving north of Foggia on the East coast of Italy. They flew the P-38 Lightning, armed with four 50-caliber machine guns (200 rounds each) and one 20mm cannon (100 rounds). The P-38 had a 260 mph cruise (mph, not knots) and could carry either two 165-gallon belly tanks or one 300-gallon belly tank and one 1,000 pound bomb. The 1st Fighter Group teamed up with the 82nd Fighter Group's P-38's to attack the oil refineries at Ploesti, Romania—and ran into a valiant and aggressive enemy. The 1st Fighter Group suffered serious losses. Here is the story, from both sides of the war:

The View from a P-38

Herb "Stub" Hatch describes the mission from his vantage point of Cragmore Green #3, the element leader of the fourth flight:

"We were briefed that morning very early. We got up around 0400, had some breakfast and went down to group headquarters for the briefing. When we walked in and sat down it was apparent that something unusual was in the air because all the group brass were in attendance. When they went to the map and drew the line to Ploesti all of us kind of went, 'Uh,oh.' And then, when they told us what the mission was, there was absolute silence and utter disbelief on the part of all of us who were going to fly over 600 miles to surprise the Germans in order to dive-bomb the Romano-Americano refinery.

"In the course of the briefing it came out that the 82nd were the ones to do the bombing. We were selected for fighter escort. I can't adequately describe the sense of relief that went through that gathering when we found out that we weren't going to be the ones carrying a 1,000 pound bomb on one side of the airplane and a belly tank on the other - or that we'd be the one's to try and dive into that unbelievable flak.

The P-38 was developed by Lockheed's early "Skunk Works" which later made the U-2, SR-71 and the F-117 Stealth Fighter. The P-38 had two-engine power, long range, and very heavy firepower.

"Take-off at 0505 went as scheduled. We rendezvoused with the 82nd and headed for the coast of Yugoslavia. Anyone who has flown formation at low level knows the difficulty in keeping a squadron of sixteen aircraft together, let alone three squadrons. Nonetheless, we hit our IP right on schedule south of Bucharest. At that point we began our turn north, dropped our belly tanks and were supposed to begin our climb to altitude to cover the 82nd. As we completed our turn however, we flew right over an enemy airfield and in the airfield pattern were four or five Dornier 217 twin-engine aircraft. Our squadron leader, First Lieutenant John Shepard turned in and went after them and three flights followed him. (Blue flight was, by this time, cut off) The Dorniers didn't last long. I only wasted some ammunition by firing at one of them at the tail end of the little fight.

"At this point we were only 250 to 300 feet off the ground. As we pulled up slightly to turn back north again somebody hollered, 'Cragmore break left for Chrissake!' I looked to my left and there was a whole flock of FW 190s headed in from ten o'clock high. [Actually Rumanian IAR 80s]

"Our entire squadron broke to the left. As I continued around in my sharp left turn a lone 190 came out of nowhere and pulled right across in front of me. He was

DO-217 German bomber

WW II: Mission to Remember Page 99

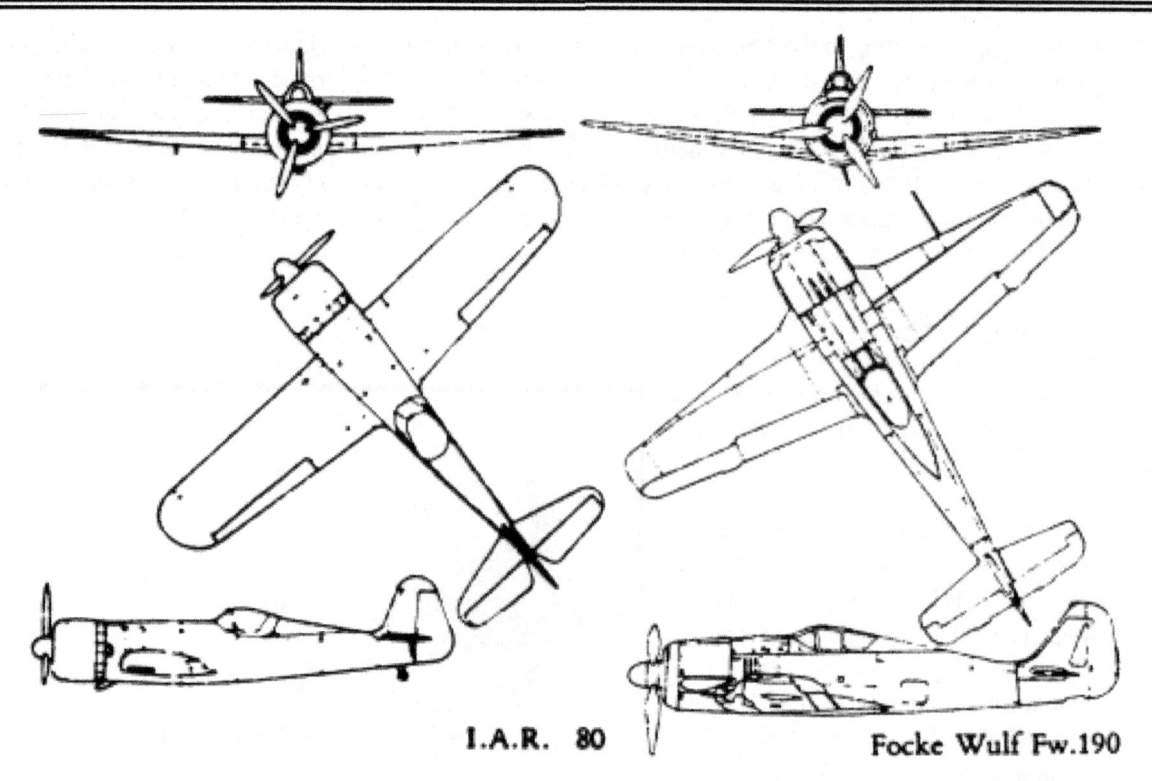

These drawings illustrate the similarity between the IAR 80 and the Focke-Wulf 190

You were shot down by a Romanian IAR 80, not a German FW-190

so close - fifty to seventy-five yards away - that all I could see in my ring sight was the belly of his fuselage and the wing roots. I opened fire with all four .50 caliber machine guns and the 20 mm cannon, and I just damn near blew him in half. That saved my neck because when I rolled out to shoot at that 190 I looked to my right and here comes another bunch of 190s from my two o'clock.

"There were four 190s in the lead. I did the only thing I could do. I turned sharply to my right, pulled up and opened fire again. The leader was 150 to 250 yards away, nearly head-on and slightly to my left. I set the lead 190 on fire with a burst that went through the engine, the left side of the cockpit and the wing root. The 190 rolled to its right and passd me on my left. I didn't see him crash but my gun camera film showed the fire and my wingman, Lieutenant Joe Morrison, confirmed that he crashed. Unfortunately the other three 190s in that flight went right over my head and down on the tails of Green flight leader and his wingman. Both were shot down.

"As I continued to turn around to my right, my wingman stayed with me and I saw another 190 right up behind one of my tentmates, Joe Jackson flying as Cragmore White #4. I closed in on that one from about his five o'clock and tried to shoot his canopy off from about 100 yards, but I was too late to save Joe. By then the 190 had set Jackson's plane on fire. Joe's plane rolled over and went in and he was killed. I finally did get my burst into the cockpit area and the 190 followed Joe right into the ground.

"I was still turning to the right, going quite slowly by then, because I had my combat flaps down. I turned maybe another ninety degrees to my right and saw one of our '38s coming head-on with a 190 on his tail. We were still around 300 feet and the P-38 passed over me by fifty to seventy-five feet. I pulled my nose up and opened fire on the trailing 190 from a distance of about 150 to 200 yards. He kept coming head-on and I shot off the bottom half of his engine. He nosed down, still shooting at me and I had to dump the yoke hard to miss him. He was burning when he went over me by not more than three feet, and part of his right wing knocked about three inches off the top of my left rudder.

"As this 190 went over my head, I saw three more making a pass at me from my left. I turned so fast I lost Joe Morrison. I missed my shot that time but when these three had gone over me (they went after Morrison) I saw three 190s diving at another P-38. I snap-shot at the leader from about a 90 degree deflection. I hit his left wing and shredded the aileron. He fell off on his wing and went in. He was so low that there was no chance for him to recover. I kept on going around to my left and shot at the second one which was going away from me on my left. I hit him, but I'm not sure if he went in. I know I knocked a bunch of pieces off his cowling and fuselage but I didn't have time to see what happened to him.

"I looked up at two o'clock and here comes another 190 right at me. It was too late for me to turn. I just shut my eyes and hunched down in the cockpit. I thought I'd bought the farm right there. But he missed me, he never even hit my ship. I think he missed me because I was going so slow. He overestimated my speed and was overleading me. I started to turn his way and, when he went behind me I continued on around. There was another one out there so I closed in on him. I took aim, fired but my guns only fired about ten rounds and quit. I was out of ammo. I damaged him a bit but he flew away.

HE-111 German Bomber

"I cannot overemphasize what a melee that was. There were at least twelve P-38s in that little area, all of them at very low altitiude. Somewhere between twenty-five and thirty 190s were also in there. None of us was at more than 200 or 300 feet and some were quite a bit lower. The topography was kind of a little hollow with some hills on each side. It was by far the wildest melee I saw in the sixty odd combat missions I flew. There were aircraft going in all over the place. I heard one guy who had been wounded pretty badly, scream until he went in. It was a wild, wild few minutes. And a few minutes is all it was. According to the mission report from our debriefing the whole fight took something like three to six minutes. I had no inkling of elapsed time while it was going on. I was too damned busy trying to stay alive.

"When I woke up to the fact that I was out of ammunition, 600 miles into enemy territory and all alone, I broke out of the area and went looking for some company. In only a few minutes I found one of the other planes in my squadron headed in my general direction. I called the pilot, Carl Hoenshell on the radio and we joined up. About that time I heard my wingman, Joe Morrison, hollering for some help. He was on single engine, pretty badly shot up and would someone please come and help him. So Hoenshell and I turned back to look for Joe. We finally found him down around 200 feet. After we got him headed in our direction we started to climb out of there to the west.

"Joe's airplane looked like a lace doily. The two 190's I had not had time to turn into had gone over the top of me and down onto Joe's tail because he had broken right when I had broken to the left. Joe's ship was flying but just barely. Hoenshell and I were both out of ammunition. The three of us tried to make ourselves as small as possible and headed west. Four or five minutes later another P-38 joined with us. This was Lieutenant John Allen, a 94th pilot. We hoped he had some ammunition. When we called to ask we found that his radio was out and we couldn't talk to him.

"Another twenty-five or thirty miles west, just as we were gaining some altitude we ran into a bunch of flak. Unfortunately Morrison became separated from us again because he couldn't maneuver as quickly as we could to get out of the flak, so we had to turn around and go back and get him again. We nursed Joe along for a long, long time. Finally we got out of Rumania and into Yugoslavia and had climbed to about 12,000 feet. We were S-ing back and forth over Joe because he couldn't fly as fast as we could on his single engine. As I was turning from one of our S'es I spotted six ME-109s about eight o'clock. I hollered to Hoenshell, `Bogies high at eight o'clock! He saw them too and cautioned, `Hold it, Hold it. Joe, hit the deck.' Joe didn't lose any time. He stuck his nose down and headed for the ground.

"Carl, Allen and I held the turn as best we could and, when the 109s broke formation and came at us from six o'clock we turned into them hoping to scare them off by looking like we were ready for a fight, but they didn't scare worth a damn. (This with no ammunition). When Hoenshell, who was leading, hollered on the radio, `Hit the deck Hatch!' I didn't waste any time doing just that. I rolled my airplane over on its back and split S'ed out of there.

"One 109 was chasing me and a couple of others were going after Hoenshell, but I don't know where the others went. There was an undercast beneath us and I didn't have the faintest idea where the hell the mountains were - Yugoslavia is full of them - but there was no choice at that point. The ME-109 was chasing me and I had nothing left to fight with so I went through that undercast so fast I didn't even see it. I was hitting close to 600 miles per hour when I came through the bottom into a valley between two high ridges. The Lord was sure with me that day. I kept going. When I was sure I'd lost the 109 I pulled back up over the overcast and started looking around for Hoenshell, Allen or Morrison, anybody. I heard Joe hollering for help but my fuel level was getting down to the point where I couldn't afford any longer to turn around and go back. I continued on toward Foggia.

"When I landed back at home base I was the first member of our squadron to return from the mission. It was noon and my elapsed time was six hours and fifty-five minutes. I don't think I had enough gas to go around again if I hadn't been able to land on my first approach. There was quite a welcoming committee at the revetment when I parked the aircraft. Shortly after I landed Cragmore Blue flight came in-all four of them. They hadn't been in the fight at all.

"Much later that evening, long after debriefing and after we seven survivors had imbibed a bit of the medicinal alcohol that the flight surgeon was kind enough to put out, who should come wandering into our officers club but Joe Morrison, my wingman. He'd gotten that lace doily across the Adriatic but had to dump it on the field at Bari. He'd hitched a ride on a truck and walked back into the squadron that evening.

"After all the smoke and dust had settled I was credited with five confirmed victories, one probable and one damaged. It's my opinion that the probable was a pretty sick puppy. I have hunch that he never flew again, but I can't prove it."

The 82nd bore the brunt of the always deadly Ploesti flak. The 1st, particularly the 71st Squadron, was caught at low altitude, at cruising speed by a large enemy force which had every advantage. In a few minutes the 71st was reduced to little more than a flight. Reviewing the chronology; when the 71st was jumped the 27th was climbing to 12, 000 feet east of Ploesti. The 94th had sailed through its covey of enemy aircraft and was climbing to join the 27th. Neither the 27th nor the 94th seemed aware of the 71st fate even at debriefing, noting only that the squadrons became separated in the target area. There was never a suggestion of turning back to assist the 71st because that would have meant abandoning the 82nd pilots. After leaving the Danube and heading toward Ploesti both groups had encountered quite a parade of enemy aircraft. The 82nd had been instructed not to engage any enemy aircraft en route but in a few cases simply couldn't avoid them. 96th Squadron pilots downed an ME-210, a Hinkel 111 and two single-engine fighters. Two other aircraft were also shot down by 82nd pilots, none of whom jettisoned their bombs or belly tanks in the process.

Despite the valiant efforts of the 1st and 82nd Fighter Groups, the results of the "experimental" June 10th low-level raid on Ploesti look meager when compared to the cost. The 1st Fighter Group lost fourteen P-38s and most of the pilots while the 82nd lost nine: a loss ratio of thirty percent.

Needless to say, the entire group was stunned by the losses incurred during the Ploesti raid. The 71st was hard pressed to field a sixteen ship squadron for the continuing escort missions. The Fifteenth Air Force evidently concluded that dive bombing attacks on heavily defended targets such as Ploesti were too costly.

Messersmitt Me-210 German twin-engine fighter.
It was unstable, slow, and generally a poor design.

The Romanian View of the Battle

Dan Vizanty gives the Romanian side of the story:

"On June 10, 1944, around 7:30 AM, after reveille, the staff of our group proceeded as usual to our headquarters. On this particular morning, I was accompanied by three Squadron leaders, Captains Petre Constantinescu, Mirecea Dumitrescu and Gheorghe Poteuca. In case of alarm, we had only two groups per squadron ready for takeoff; i.e. 24 planes without staff planes, altogether a total of 26 planes.

"The Air Force headquarters for the Balkans in Otoperi (a small forest, six miles north of Bucharest) had the code name "Tiger". The headquarters was under the command of the German Colonel Eduard Neumann. The air raids of the American Air Force into Romania had never taken place before 10:00 AM. But on this morning, something extraordinary happened. At 8:00 A.M. the alarm sirens went off! Amazed about the unusual hour I grabbed my alarm pistol and fired 'green' for my units, the order for immediate take-off. Then my aide, Lt. Puiu Lupescu, and I headed for our staff planes. After one minute and 36 seconds the first squadron started. I had long ago made a specific battle plan for this kind of situation.

"Immediately after takeoff the fighters had to climb in a tight spiral to an altitude of 4600 feet directly over the airfield. My aide and I took off immediately following the last squadron, cutting across the curve of their ascent, taking the lead position in the group. We continued to climb, reaching a previously fixed sector (sector SN) 63 miles north of Bucharest where we generally arrived at an altitude of 30,000 feet. We had flown this maneuver very often and knew it well. During the climb I would receive on the radio all necessary information about the American attack from the headquarters "Tiger" in Otoperi, like direction and altitude of each wave of bombers, their most likely destination and such.

"This morning however, while crossing the flight path of the ascending fighters to take the lead at 4600 feet, I heard in my headset: 'Attention Paris, Attention Paris, turkeys over the nest.' I recognized the voice of Traian Garriliu, chief of the command post at the airport Papesti/Leordeni telling me that the American fighter planes (turkeys) were heading for the airport (nest). Simultaneously I could see, at very low altitude, wave upon wave of Lightning fighter planes with twin bombs coming from the east, heading straight for our airport.

"Wihout hesitation I radioed: "Paris to Paris 1,2,3 (my groups – squadrons?) we attack, follow me! In seconds, the tables turned: instead of the surprise planned by the Americans for us by flying at the lowest possible altitude from Foggia over the Adriatic Sea and Jugoslavia along the Dona River to Oltenitza, we fell upon them, taking them into a tight squeeze before they could even begin their first attack. Our Blitz attack was a total surprise for the Lightning fighters. Indeed all my pilots, like one man, dove down onto the American planes—one after the other."

"The surprise was unbelievable. Like a thunderstorm we drove them ahead of us. I have to admit that our first attack was the decisive one and this it was our luck to shoot down the commander of the unit during the first moments of the fight. He was the only survivor of the American pilots who took part in this attack. Our attack was so fast that not one of the hundred American planes managed to fire a shot on our planes still on the ground."

"It was easy to distinguish the participants in this air battle: on one side the twin fuselage Lightnings, on the other side the IAR 80, made any mix-up impossible. The low altitude at which this fight took place made the battle so difficult. It all took place near the ground and not higher than 615 feet, in total confusion. Completely surprised, half of the American planes tried to retreat. By using the technique of circle of defense, they succeeded to leave our area and return to Foggia.

"With keyed up nerves, wide-awake and fully aware I took in the whole scene of the air battle. Excited and proud I looked down at my good tough old planes, the IAR 80s who came out winners thanks to their extraordinary maneuverability. I watched their crazy dives, their quick rolls, their U-turns and upside-down flights. They fired only very short bursts to conserve ammunition. A indescribably sight but what a drama for the Lightnings which, at this low altitude, were definitely the underdog to the ever-present, quick IAR 80s.

"The people on the ground stood petrified looking at the sky. Farmers in the fields, workers of the textile factory "Apertura" located next to the airfield, and of course our own technical air base personnel, all were witnesses and spectators of the battle in the bright summer sunshine of the tremendous noise of the explosions, the rat-tat-tat of the machine guns, the whining of the engines and in between, everywhere the white smoke spirals of the burning, crashing planes. Then sudden quiet—only the droning of the again calmly running engines. A battle of twelve minutes, horribly long for one, unbelievably short for the other. We flew home to land trying to fly again in a closed formation.

"Such was the way the air battle ended: one of the most important and remarkable ones of the Second World War on the southeast front. Twenty-four shot-down American planes were counted in the immediate vicinity of the airfield Polesti/Leordeni. Regrettably only one American pilot survived, the commander of the unit. He had succeeded in getting out of the plane before it exploded after an emergency landing."

"Our ground personnel gave us a triumphal welcome when we landed. They lifted us out of the planes, embraced us and cried with joy and excitement.

IAR-80, Romania's best WW II Fighter
Note similarity to the German FW-190

"After the first excitement subsided, we realized with sadness three of our comrades were missing. Lt. Limburg whose nickname was 'General' who collided during the battle with the two adjutants Tari and Giurgin, both shot down by the Americans. This fact brought us cruelly back down to earth to look at our own losses. The amazing thing was that all of us had returned safely to our base in spite of many bullet holes in our planes. I noticed with surprise a hole in my windshield where a 13.2-mm bullet had entered and gone into the fuselage. The trajectory of this bullet should have taken it through my head. None of us could explain how and by what miracle I was still alive. I find this fact one of the extraordinary and unexplainable events of this day."

Dan Vizanty

Dan Vizanti thought the target was his own airfield near Bucharest. He was unaware of the entire 82nd Group and that the real target was the Ploesti refinery. With at least three languages involved some of the exaggerated statistics can be overlooked, but Vizanty was right about one thing. They caught the 71st by surprise and cut it to pieces. Vizanty indicated that the normal practice of his unit, once an alert was sounded, was to take-off and climb to about 30,000 feet by which time they would be positioned some sixty-three miles north of Bucharest. On this morning they had taken off and reached about 4,600 feet when they were alerted and, "saw the Lightnings approaching at low altitude from the east with twin bombs." [Presumably the twin bombs were belly tanks or the twin booms of the P-38 tail] Vizanty goes on to say, "it was our luck to shoot down the commander of the unit [which they did not do]. Our attack was so fast that not one of the hundred American planes managed to fire a shot on our planes still on the ground." An interesting defenders point of view. Vizanty's 100 American Lightnings were, in reality, three flights of 71st Squadron ships, twelve P-38s. As a defender he missed the entire 82nd Fighter Group and two squadrons of the 1st Fighter Group.

IAR-80 Romanian Fighter - painting

The Spirit of Attack

American P-47 Thunderbolt was similar to the IAR-80 and FW-190. Air-cooled radial engines were less vulnerable than liquid-cooled in-line engines, which would fail if a bullet cut a coolant line. There was armor behind the pilot, and the P-47 became known as our toughest fighter.

Focke-Wulf FW-190, model

The Spirit of Attack

An F-102 of the 317th Fighter Interceptor Squadron, piloted by Dean Rands, flies near Mt. McKinley, Alaska, in 1963. I took this photo while flying my F-102, holding the control stick between my knees and the camera with my hands. I love this photo because it shows the wild terrain of Alaska and the vast airspaces where we could maneuver without restrictions and hone our skills in this beautiful but dangerous airspace.

When my wife picked up enlargements at the Base Exchange, the clerk asked: "Where was your husband standing when he took that picture?"

I conclude this book with a salute to the pilots of all nations who have put their lives on the line in defense of their countries. Fighter pilots are a select group who must be technically skilled, brave, sharp-eyed, and aggressive. They must have the spirit of attack. I am deeply proud of having been honored to fly with them.

CPSIA information can be obtained
at www.ICGtesting.com
Printed in the USA
BVOW07s1133190717
489710BV00003B/41/P